Journey of a Gypsy Soul

Elizabeth A. Kogut

Elizabeth A. Kogut

ISBN: 978-1-952263-95-8

Dedication

This book is dedicated to Lorna, my true friend, who has inspired me over the last 32 years of my life. She is a mother-figure to me and has been there through the darkest days of my life to the happiest days.

To Kyle, my beloved son and only child. He's the love of my life, my pride, my joy, and even my rock at times. I believe words can never describe the love that I have for my son.

God bless him!

Acknowledgment

Writing a book is harder than I thought, and more rewarding than I could have ever imagined. It was indeed a surreal process, and none of this would have been possible without all of you I am about to mention.

I want to start by thanking Lorna, my awesome friend and Mother, who inspires me always, and she is as important to this book getting done as I am. To Janet Adams, another mother-figure who was another wonderful inspiration for getting this book completed. Thank you, Kyle, my son, who is the most important person in my life. I am always proud of you.

Thanks to everyone on my publishing team who worked so diligently on the book content, cover, and marketing. You all did an amazing job! I'm grateful for your editorial help, keen insight, and ongoing support in bringing my story to life. It is because of your efforts and encouragement that I have a legacy to pass on to my family, where one did not exist before.

To my family: my sisters, Cathy and Gail, thank you for taking this journey with me through some dark, desperate years and happy times. You motivate me to be the best sister I can be.

To my biological Mom, Sharon, thank you for bringing me into this world. I am happy I got to reunite with you and to have taken you peacefully into your final journey.

To my sisters, Barbara and Rita, I finally got to meet you and share a very intimate time with our mother's passing and hope to see more of you over the years.

I would also like to acknowledge my foster parents, George and Evelyn Edge, who took me in as a broken foster child and raised me to be a caring, compassionate person.

To all my loves along the way, you all taught me how to love and become a better person.

To all my employers, who taught me to grow in my profession of nursing over the last 30 years!

To all my dear friends, too many to mention that I have met along the way in my journey who helped me grow and experience all facets of life, love, friendships, and travel.

About the Author

Elizabeth Kogut is a travel nurse who has years of professional experience under her name. She has always enjoyed traveling and meeting new people. She started her career joining the Navy Marine Corps. She spent a lot of time in the Navy, and had a son during that period. At a young age, Elizabeth, the eldest, along with her siblings, was adopted by a couple. She remained strong, raised her younger siblings, and achieved one milestone after another. This is Elizabeth's first book out of the many more to come!

Preface

I was part of the foster care system, but it wasn't the choice I made. As a matter of fact, no child makes that choice, but one can't stand against fate. It doesn't matter how we start our lives, but what matters is how we direct it. I worked hard to achieve my goals. Today, I am glad where I am.

There were up's and down's; there were mistakes I made, and thus faced the consequences. But that is what life is all about, rising, falling, and doing it all over again. One of the significant reasons for sharing my story is to let you know that no matter how difficult life seems, you always have the potential to rise above it. Many people will enter your life and leave it, but your only family remains by your side, till your last breath. I never forced myself to become a different person than I was; I always followed my heart, and so even today, my gypsy soul is just as excited to take on new adventures, as it was since my childhood.

Contents

Contents

Chapter 1
Early Childhood with Biological Parents

We all know the old saying, *"You can't pick your parents."* We are all sent to this world with the basic need for shelter, food, and love. However, more often than not, these basic needs are not met for one reason or another. The reason for my parents not catering to those basic needs is what made my early life a challenge.

All children out there are more or less the same. They are honest and sensitive. It is abhorrent to use them for worldly gains, no matter how basic they appear to be. It was something too complicated for my parents to understand, and it wasn't just them who suffered but also the children they had brought into this world.

Speaking of it as a victim makes me question my parents' idea of starting a family. My birth was not my choice, but it sure was theirs. If they weren't sure how they were to take care of us, they shouldn't have started a family in the first place. Nevertheless, amongst the various things life has taught me, one of them is to accept things as they exist while taking responsibility for the future. I have learned not to stress over something I have no control over.

I was born in the Burroughs of Queens, NY. It was a project for people with low incomes. At least, that was how we knew it. We lived on the eleventh floor of the project. I was the first child my parents had, and then I was followed by three younger siblings. Basically, since my birth, my parents had a kid every year. Of course, there were perks of being the first child of the family. I was spoiled at the beginning by my parents and people in my extended family. I was loved by all of my aunts, uncles, and cousins, but little did I know that my childhood days were going to get over before my childhood.

I was just three years old when my parental instincts came into play. Yes, it's a very young age to experience such things, but I guess God has his ways of keeping us alive. Otherwise, my siblings and I might have never made it into our teens, let alone growing old. One of the main reasons why I matured before time was because of my parents. They were rarely around, and even when they were, it was complete chaos as we the kids would switch to survival mode. I never wanted to have whereabouts of life at an age as young as three, but it was my circumstances that did not leave me with a choice. Survival is a trait we have by default, and that was what encouraged me to protect myself and my younger siblings. Parents and protection are synonymous, aren't they? In our case, unfortunately, they were antonyms.

I certainly did not have loving role models to educate or guide me, that too in times when we as children needed it the most. Maybe, some of us are born with stronger survival skills than others. My memory has several incidents to prove how adamantly my survival skills were all that came to my rescue. My parents were so careless in raising their children that by the time I turned five, they had lost all their parental rights.

I am not fond of dwelling into the past, and well, why would I? After all, the memories are nightmares that I hope to forget. The memories don't haunt me anymore, but their presence is never comforting. For instance, the time my mother, along with a male figure (not my Dad), took me to the boardwalk by our home. I remember it as if it wasn't decades ago, but yesterday. She placed me on a mechanical horse, put the quarter in, and walked away out towards the beach. What followed after was heinous. I vividly remember my Mom and the man arguing over something when my Mom was suddenly hurled over the railing and down to the beach below. Unable to understand what was happening, I sat on the horse in a state of shock that lasted until the man came to me. He got me off the horse, and we ran home, which was not far away. As we were briskly approaching home, the man constantly attempted to convince me not to let my Mom in when she arrived. I just looked at him, not saying but thinking *I will help her.*

To wait for Mom to reach the apartment door seemed longer than eternity. As soon as she arrived, she banged on the door. I looked out the window to see her wet, cold, and shivering. All she pleaded was "*Let me in*" while tears rolled down her face. I couldn't resist, and so, I ran to the door to let her in. Before I could make it to the door, I felt a beer bottle crash into my lower back. It left a scar I carry to this day.

The pain got me off my feet to my knees as I crawled toward the door. There was blood coming down my back, but that did not stop me from letting Mom in. It was a very long night, which I spent weeping in pain while my mother

4

and her friend argued through the wee hours of the morning. It was the first time I felt a sense of responsibility. I did not know what I was going to do, but I did not let the man get away with his emotional and physical actions towards her. Letting my mother in by standing against what was wrong made me think over matters differently. All in all, I was just three years old.

As children, my siblings and I were neglected every day. None of us were old enough to know how to react to such situations. I being the eldest, decided to change things for my younger siblings. I was going to make sure that my siblings were loved and cared for by me, if not anyone else. I guess I saw glimpses of loving and caring briefly through my extended family, which was the only source of my grooming at the time. Even though our meetups with our extended family were quite scarce, it was all that we had to cherish. I often wished that they visited more often, only because we were left alone quite frequently to feed and bathe ourselves at such a young age.

I took care of that to the best of my ability. Although it might not have been sufficient, given I was a child myself, I did as much as possible.

My parents did not adore my baby blue eyes, but I had to use them to beg. Tears were the only weapon I had to convince people for donations. There were times when I even had to dumpster dive to make sure we did not starve.

I remember the dumpster behind a Dunkin Donuts outlet that had a boxful of day-old donuts. It was a real treat to us. One night, while I was getting some donuts out of the dumpster, the owner spotted me and invited me inside. She said, *"Come inside with me. I am tired of watching you here every night."* She gave me a fresh box of donuts and asked me to come inside from then on. She promised that she would make sure we had fresh donuts from that day. To this day, it amazes me that everyone did not want to get involved with reporting abuse or neglect but would do their part to help whenever they could.

The grocery store was another place that had to be visited regularly for survival. Believe it or not, I was not that bad of a thief as nobody at the store caught me for a long time. All I stole was bread, milk, cereal, and cheese. The world was a different place then. Today, if I find a 4-year-old roaming around grabbing a few items, I would sure investigate. It's not that I wouldn't assist, but the curiosity wouldn't let me ignore such actions of a kid. Thinking back now, I believe that the grocery store attendants knew what I did and just let it happen. Eventually, the day came when a manager caught me. Not knowing how to react, I quickly dropped the groceries and ran for my life. All the incident did was make me change grocery stores.

Desperation had the best of me for understandable reasons. My parents were uneducated, and I am not saying it to degrade them. That is what the truth is. They were battling a few drug addictions while continuing to have more children. Was it not too much to do? I learned through my own life experiences that addictions lead to poor choices. It always seems like an uphill battle that never gets easier. Money is what controls everything, and the absence of it does not leave us with another choice but to work for it. Put the blame on capitalism or support it with your theory; living without money can be way more torturous than most of us assume. Some people have emotional support to balance their financial shortcomings. We lacked both.

We had a rundown home with actual holes in the roof and areas of the floor. The living room was in the worst state. Running out of specific ideas that did not require any hard work, my mother came up with a temporary solution. She proposed to throw me down the hole so she could sue the landlord for the damage. Desperation does make you do crazy things. Her craziness had breached all boundaries. She did not even think of the consequences of injuring her child.

Many of you might have read books on a mother's love. I was so unlucky that I couldn't find it even when I was with her. After I had my son, it made it all the more difficult for me to comprehend my mother's behavior toward her children. Motherhood is sacred, and nobody has the right to abuse it. I wish I could have it any other way.

Anyway, I was thrown down a two-story hole, breaking a few ribs and my ankle. It was unbelievable, but my parents got away with their story at the hospital. According to the plan, they even managed to sue the landlord. The money they got through the lawsuit was used by them to take us, kids, to the harbor for a boat ride. We needed clothes, shoes, and whatnot, but the boat ride was of most importance for my mother.

My only focus then was to provide for my siblings. This one stormy night, when I returned from the grocery store, my siblings requested for grill cheese sandwiches for dinner.

By then, it had become a part of my routine to make dinner and give baths to my younger siblings. I also read bedtime stories to put them to sleep. Since I wasn't tall enough to reach the stove, I had to place a chair to be able to reach the stove. I turned on the gas stove after putting butter on the bread slices, not realizing that a kitchen towel was lying near the flame. Before I knew it, the kitchen was up in flames.

Scared to see fire and smoke all around the house, I ran out of the kitchen to locate my siblings as smoke started to fill the rooms of the house. In the meantime, I heard the sirens and fire trucks coming down the street. Gladly, all of us got out safely.

At that time, there were no adults in the home, as often was the case. Finally, a near-tragedy alarmed the authorities that four young children were alone and severely neglected. It was then that we were taken away by social services; it was the day when my life changed.

Chapter 2
The Foster Care System

Everything was happening so quickly that it was tough for me to cope up with the situation. Being the eldest sibling, I was the one interviewed by authorities. I was very grown-up for a four-year-old, and it was all because of my circumstances. I let them know it had been several days since we had an adult at home and that I was looking after my siblings to the best of what I could. They looked at each other in disbelief. I did find out later that the newspapers revealed our situation to be the worst neglect case NY had ever seen in a long time!

At this point, I had a lot of questions such as, *"would we ever see our parents again, or where are we going."* What bothered me the most was being separated from my siblings. The thoughts scared me, as the parental instincts in me couldn't let go of the negativity rooting in my mind. There was a strong feeling in my heart that we would not make it without each other. The love for my siblings was all I had, and I didn't want it to be taken away.

The wait at the police station was very long. We were waiting for officials from the social service department to arrive. The nice people at the police station got us some food and drinks, which helped a great deal in killing time. My siblings were oblivious to the whole situation, and it seemed that as long as we were together, no chaos could bring them into a state of panic.

A gray-haired lady, probably in her fifties, finally arrived. The glasses she wore made her look very graceful. She put us all in a car and spoke very few words. I guess she thought we were all too young to understand what was about to happen. We finally pulled up to a huge house that had a lot of windows. As we walked through the big front door, we were greeted by what they called the house mother. She was an old lady who was extremely sweet and soft-spoken. It did not take me long to comprehend that it was a group home with many foster children living there. What we all had in common was our wait for a permanent home.

The infamous orphanage was named "Angel Guardian Home." They were truly Angels to us. Although getting accustomed to the new lifestyle had my primary attention, the concerns of being separated from my siblings never left my mind. The thought would make room for pure panic to set in, as my heart raced, failing to hold the tears back. I remember saying to the house mother, *"Please keep us all together."* She promised that they would do the best they could.

Life at the group home was nice, specifically in regard to the life we had been living. That place taught us sharing with others, and I even got to be more like the child I was. Playtime was the most fun part of the day. I had a hard time transitioning from the "little mommy" to "big sister" role. I still found myself helping with the everyday caring of my siblings. They were very close to me and were shy with adults helping out. We all had rules to follow and chores to complete, even at such a young age. It was the place where we learned our first set of values. Before living in a foster home, we didn't even know the value and meaning of simple words like "Please" and "Thank you." It was how hard our domestic life had been.

I was too young to keep track of time, but it seemed months had passed when we had a visit from our mother. It was a supervised visit with social services. I remember she brought a young man with her who was not our father. So all

I could think was that our real Dad had gone out of our lives forever. It led to more confusion, and I was unable to understand other people's purpose in our lives. I just embraced whatever help I could receive from my younger siblings, but trust was a huge factor that seemed unachievable.

So anyway, my mother brought small gifts and ice-cream that hot summer day to the group home. I remember her saying, *"I am trying really hard to get you, kids, back, but I promise you all will be coming home soon."* Of course, I did not know what was entailed until years later, when I worked with the CPS. We had several visits from our mother, besides the visits from several families that tried to separate us by taking us to different foster homes. After all, four children at once could be quite a feat. I fought the constant battle of "keeping us together."

One warm sunny Saturday, our mother somehow earned the privilege to take us out for a short drive to have lunch. The day started smoothly, and everything seemed to be in place when suddenly our mother was speeding, trying to outrun the police and their sirens. We were all sitting in the back seat, not able to understand what was happening. My mother was breaking the law and trying to take us over state lines! We were caught before anyone was hurt.

A few weeks later, we were sitting in the front area of the courtroom as our mother was being charged with kidnapping and loss of all parental rights. We officially became "Award of the Court" and remained in foster care for the rest of our lives. We were not allowed to move out of it until we turned eighteen years old. I remember crying and screaming, "Mommy," as we left the courtroom. She could only wave and blow kisses with tears streaming down her face. None of us knew what fate had planned until thirty-five years later.

After the court incident, the future seemed very uncertain. As to how things had been, I only believed that more trouble would follow. The fear of the future always kept me on guard on each decision I had to take. Our long journey with foster care had begun. In the passage of four years, we went to about eight foster homes. Each time we went to a new home, I was given the social worker's business card. Even at a young age, I could call anytime for help. I was told that if I found myself in an abusive situation, I just had to make the call. I unfortunately had to do that several times.

Taking all four of us was difficult for most families to handle. I thought back then with the treatment we received that they took us in for the money. Some foster homes had other and older children who abused us in different ways, both emotionally and physically. The emotional side, as I found out over the years, hurts more than the physical, as the physical scars go away, but the emotional ones never do. I had to watch out for my younger siblings constantly, so in a way, my role of being a young parent continued!

I was sick and tired of constantly hearing, *"your mother did not want you; what is wrong with you." "My mother and father will never be your Mom and Dad," "you are just here so we can get money." "No one will ever love you, "you will live with many families, so don't get comfortable."* A few families portrayed bizarre behavior at mealtimes, and there were times when we were not allowed to sit at the table. We had to get in a line and be spoon-fed, even when we were just 2-5 years of age. We were not only spoon-fed but treated miserably. If it was your turn again and you had not swallowed the food yet, they force-fed until you eventually vomited it all up. Then, of course, we were punished.

Some of the punishments included standing in a corner with knees bent until it hurt so bad that we fell over. We were then kicked around until we got back up and started over. We were also put in small closets for very long periods. It seemed like days would pass before we were taken out. But I did not tolerate that for long as I called the social worker to get us out of there. Of course, the foster parents denied it, but the officials of the social services believed me. Such a small child couldn't make up such stories, after all.

Over the next three years, we were sent to several foster homes, but none of them worked. We always ended up going back to the group home. We were all a little older by then, and so I went back to being a kid since we had adults there to take of us. It's not that they were just following protocols, but in fact, the staff actually cared. I guess that is where I first learned what compassion is. We continued in the group home as many families came through and tried to separate us. There were times when a family would only volunteer to pick one of us, but I would never let their proposal be accepted. I fought and was determined that we were going to be together and believe it or not; it worked!

I had lost any home in finding a family that genuinely treated us right and were not there just for the money. Finally, on a bright morning, an older lady and her twenty-year-old daughter came in and decided to take all four of us. God Bless Them! They lived in Long Island, NY, which was a two to three-hour drive from New York City. I remember the daughter saying, *"Dad will be surprised when he gets home! We are bringing four children home."* My foster Dad worked at Ryker's Island prison system in NY. My foster mother stayed home and took care of the house and family. As we pulled up to this gigantic two-story home, I remember thinking, *"Wow, what a beautiful home."*

We pulled into a long driveway alongside the house on the right side. It had a big lawn in the front yard and an above ground pool in the back. It was a beautiful neighborhood, and my school was only five blocks away. We got out of the car and ran into the house through the back door that led into a big kitchen. I still remember the layout of the house and all the rooms in it. It was a four-bedroom, two-bath home. We continued to go through this beautifully furnished home room by room. There was a huge dining room that led to a huge living room. When we saw the neat couches, we immediately started to jump all over the furniture for some reason. We were quickly halted by a stern voice of our new foster mother "*that is for sitting, now sit down, it looks like we have to go over a few rules!*"

We continued exploring the house, moving onto the second floor. There was a big bathroom on the right at the top of the stairs. The first door on the right after the bathroom was a smaller bedroom for my brother. Then there were three more bedrooms, including the master bedroom. I, along with my two sisters, stayed in one room with bunk beds. We were quite happy with that. Our foster father, on our first day, was still at work. We all sat down to have a late lunch, and we got to sit at a table, but we still had to learn the proper way of using the silverware. Well, it wasn't difficult, so we quickly learned it.

We had another issue of eating too fast as we were rushed in the group foster home, or we would not get to eat. We slowly learned to enjoy our food. When our foster father came home, he looked at us in surprise. I will never forget the look on his face seeing so many of us. He said, "*Wow, what have you done? I guess you are the one that stays at home; they will keep you busy.*"

By this time, I was about eight years old and had never been to school yet. We moved so much from one home to another that the chaos never spared me the stability to start school. I was tested out of kindergarten and went straight to first grade, but was still two years behind. But it sure seemed better late than never. My other siblings needed to get to school, too, and we were all behind. We had to start learning how to trust others in our lives, and at this point, I was finally able to be the kid of my age. It was hard for me to transition, but my foster mother helped me a great deal. She actually appreciated it, especially at bath and bedtime. We did have social worker visits, but this home so far was the best. At the age of eleven, we moved to another part of New York and still had access to social workers. The visits were to check on our safety and wellbeing.

It was getting tense in the home as we grew older and needed more time from our foster parents. Also, my foster father had finally retired from law enforcement. He did not have as much patience with us as our foster mother did. We had this camp in upstate New York that we visited in the summer, and we also would spend some of those three months of summer in the Catskill Mountains of upstate New

York. We were always gone all summer engaged in camping, swimming, hayrides, and even barn dances with every night barbeque. We met other kids of our age and would just run amuck! For the first time in our lives, we were actually having fun.

Chapter 3
My Teenage Years

When I turned 13 years old, it was time to move upstate New York. The camp was torn down, and a beautiful log cabin was built. It was the retirement time of my foster parents and the beginning of my teenage years. The log cabin was beautiful; it had a full basement where my foster mother did ceramics and all her canning. Some of her exquisite products were tomato sauce, apple butter, pickles, and jellies. We were not allowed to eat them but had eaten enough to know they were a delicious treat.

The living room was sunken in with a big fireplace. There was a loft over the living room, which was my brother's bedroom. We, the three girls, shared a large bedroom. The property had an outhouse that was part of the original campsite, the outhouse I haven't been able to forget. By the end of the first year, I realized I no longer had the opportunity to reach a social worker. It was like once we moved upstate New York, we were cut off from communication and so getting in touch with social services was no more possible.

The environment in the home became violent and abusive emotionally, physically, and sexually. My only brother at the time started running away from this foster home as he could not take the abuse we were enduring each day. The authorities had to bring him in over and over again. Somehow we could never get the help we needed, while our foster parents advertised us as ill-mannered children.

One day my brother ran away, and they just stopped looking for him. Later I found out that he took a wrong path, subsequently spending a long time in prison. The emotional abuse began impacting my life negatively. I began isolating myself from the rest of the family to the extent that I could not eat with or talk to them. It was the saddest form of punishment for me as I had to stay distant from people that I had become close with. After all, we shared many experiences and had developed a liking for each other.

It was a difficult time for me, but having gone through worse, I managed to have the motivation to cope up with the situation. Although, then, I was terribly failing. I felt sad and lonely. Often times, I wondered if I really deserved the life I was living. Happiness, trust, and comfort don't come easily, but it was too difficult for me to understand it in my early teens. Life is already confusing when you become a teenager, with all the hormonal growth and awareness of newer realities. On top of all that, the stress of being alone and unable to understand why life mistreated me, made the circumstances unbearable.

I also thought I was going to be strong and not let anyone tear me down! It didn't really help me either; in fact, it worked against me, making me a little rebellious at times. Basically, I had shifted the entire focus of my foster parents on myself. I did so to take all the abuse and leave less of it for my younger sisters – it was only the three of us left.

On a lighter note, it's not that we never learned something constructive from our foster parents. They taught us work-ethics and discipline. My foster father would always say, *"All I have is three girls who will be better than any three boys!"* We would help tie down and cut trees for firewood. I remember the sap being so sticky.

Since it was very cold in upstate NY, we learned how to shovel a lot of snow. The log cabin was on top of a big hill with a very steep driveway. Many times we would get home from school while Mom and Dad would be out running errands. So we would surprise them by having the whole driveway shoveled for them to drive up easier. My Dad also taught us how to drive the small jeep with a plow attached.

We were very active in all four seasons. In the summers, we would ride our bikes down to the lake, which was about three miles one way. We lived on a rural road with houses spread about a mile apart, and the end of the road led to a beautiful lake. It had a dam, and we would jump off of it and swim for hours.

There was a big apple tree down by the lake from where we picked apples for Mom so she could make applesauce and apple butter. It was a happy childhood for several years until I became a teenager. Ever since then, things never got back to normal. Once I switched to survival mode, I never found the opportunity to switch it off until I left the house after graduating from High School.

It all started one day when my Mom was going to the store and left me home with my Dad. It was when I began hating the outhouse we had. We lived in the outhouse before the nice log cabin was built. When my Mom wasn't home, my Dad lured me into the outhouse and wanted me to perform oral sex on him. He said things like, *"You will like this," "It will feel good," and "This is our little secret that you can never tell anyone."*

At first, I couldn't make sense of the situation. I would ask him what the hell was wrong with him. I would fight him as he would try to force my head down. He would get rough, and I would usually get away. I would always beg Mother to take me with her when she ran errands. I did get to go most of the time. There was a strain between myself and my 55-year-old foster father.

I would stay as far away as I could from him. I joined every sport in school, played three instruments, and even sang in the chorus just to be away from home as much as I could. As the memories reappear in my mind, they bring disgust and agony with them. My plans of remaining occupied at school worked for me but angered him as his chances to assault me had decreased. I was always on my guard throughout my entire teenage. He did manage to punish me in whatever brutal way he could. It got me isolated from the family. My siblings were not allowed to speak to me, and I had to eat alone most of the time.

I fail to understand how my Mom allowed this brutal punishment to be carried out. Maybe, she was afraid of him, just as I was. My Mom and I did have our differences, and so to say, I would push buttons at times as all teenagers do. If I looked at her the wrong way or answered in the wrong tone, I was usually punished with physical abuse, but as usual, I fought back, which would only make it worse. It was a frequent scenario to be chased down the hallway to my bedroom. I always got there first and so would lock the door. He would bang on the door, screaming, *"Open this door, or I will tear it off the hinges."* I would reply, *"I will be here waiting when you get the door down!"*

I was a fighter and was not going to let him have an easy time getting to me. When he would get to me, he would totally be exhausted but very angry and adrenaline-driven. He would bruise me with a punch or hit me with a switch. I, too, gave him some bruises in return fighting back with my fists and kicking him during the altercations. I often bit him given a chance and would never let him get the best of me.

I ran away on several occasions hoping they would eventually take me to juvenile hall and that I would never have to return there again. It wasn't going to be easy either, as I had to make sure my siblings left the house with me. I was still trying to protect them as they were punished, too, but in a less severe way.

One evening, I ran away in a snow storm. It was 10 degrees outside with a wind chill factor of negative 20. I was nicely covered as we had a lot of winter gear courtesy to the area of the country we lived in. Although I wasn't keeping track of time, it seemed like hours had passed. It kept on getting colder, and my feet had frostbite making every passing second difficult than the previous one. I could feel the tingling and pain in my toes and feet. I finally found the road that was plowed, as the blowing wind was piercing through my body and stinging my face. After a while, my body had become numb, and just when I thought I couldn't walk another inch, I saw lights and sirens of a police car with my foster Dad following behind. My first thought was a horrific one, *"Oh My God, I have to go back to that house and get beaten,"* but it did not last for long. At that point, my brain had stopped functioning as my body hurt so badly.

I was told to get into the warm car or was rather helped into it. When I sat in the car, it was discovered that I had frostbite on my toes. I was escorted into the nice warm house by the nice policeman. He asked the entire family to sit in the living room so he could explain the dangers of running away. He also told us how we could eventually go to the juvenile hall and not be returned to the family.

My younger sisters were scared and did not want to lose me after losing Mom. I was trying to be their rock but fell short sometimes. My frostbite was treated; I drank my hot chocolate and went to bed. I was extremely exhausted and instantly went to sleep. My Dad waited to punish me the next day, and so he did. I had to sit in my room alone all day with no meals. It seemed like quite a harsh punishment, but food and isolation seemed to be a punishment of choice.

The lines of punishment with or without food included several scenarios that were becoming quite a pattern. The favorite theme seemed to be that the refrigerator and cabinets had locks on them, so after school, we could not have a snack as most kids do! So we would break into the neighbor's houses as they were only summer camps and steal whatever food we could find. Even if it were stale donuts, we wouldn't mind having them, and in all honesty, they tasted good to us.

We were not proud of stealing, but it was just another survival tactic for us. We were always very hungry. The really sad part is that the neighbors, upon their return in the summer, would report the numerous break-ins. We would hear our foster mother on the gossip line, appalled by such behavior, and nobody in a million years suspected us.

It was so sad to hear our foster mother talk about it to others. Ironically, she would say things like, *"All they take is food; they must be hungry," "Who would deprive others of food?"* We would be in our bedroom, saying, *"YOU do!"* I would have the urge to run out of the room, pull the phone from her, and tell our neighbors the real truth. Everyone needed to know the monster they both would become at times.

She had us painted as hellions while we were just trying to be loved and treated with respect. The neighbors thought that foster children are all broken and disrespectful. I don't blame them for that. It is amazing how they painted such a horrible picture of us despite all their injustice. If the neighbors knew the truth, they would never have considered us as ungrateful or disrespectful kids.

Now, the '70s was a very different era. Maybe, we weren't socially as mature as we are now. To what I saw and observed, it was a time when grown-ups did not want to report any child abuse or neglect. For them, it was about minding their own business, so most people stayed out of it. I personally would share my stories and request my teachers and bus drivers to help us get out of the abusive situation. None ever did anything to help my siblings or me. As I said, they just minded their own business. I hope times have changed for others, and people respond to the ones in need of assistance against any and every kind of abuse.

The extracurricular activities had me occupied in school and consumed all evenings of the week. I would get home late each night, go to bed, and repeat it the next day. I did feel a sense of belonging on all my sports teams and had great friends to spend time with. I could not and did not share the abuse with them, fearing to lose the only friends I had. I needed to hang on to the little joy and happiness that I felt.

In my junior year, while playing soccer, I managed to break both bones in my lower right leg. I was playing defense, and it was a championship game with our biggest rivalries at the time. In fact, their teammate had kicked me on purpose. I fell to the ground in excruciating pain, and as I looked down at my leg, it was bowed out like a bubble. The coaches put a soft blown up splint around it, and I was rushed to the hospital.

Prior to all that, I told my sister, who played center on the team, to win the game for us. I also told her to have a few choice words with the one who kicked me! I went on to the hospital and waited in the ER till what seemed forever. The holdup involved some politics with foster care getting permission to treat me or even give me a Tylenol for that matter. The team, in the meantime, did win the game with my sister kicking the winning goal. The team came to the ER with a big pizza party even though I was being prepped for surgery. They did not actually cut open my leg, but rather manipulated the bones. They twisted it up to my thigh for six months in a plaster cast to allow it to heal on its own. Oh boy, it did start stinking and itching after a while!

The cast weighed more than I did, and it made me fall out of bed numerous times as I tossed and turned, trying to get sleep with the extra weight. We lived on a huge hill to get to our beautiful one-story log home. I welcomed winter, walking on crutches. I was teased because the short bus came up the hill to the front door to pick me up. Of course, at school, I had all my friends assist me in my classes, and they even carried my books. I attended a few school dances and other fundraising events with the cast on.

Then the day finally came, and it was time to get rid of the cast. For one thing, many pairs of my boots and shoes were ruined due to wear and tear on one shoe or boot. Also, I will never forget when the cast was removed – the stench was overwhelming. I had a thick white film of dead skin on the right leg, and my leg was about as round as my small wrist. It took hours to scrub it off, not to mention the five razors I used to shave that leg. It took months to build up the muscle in that leg, but it was quite an experience.

When I turned 17, my foster parents did something very nice for me. They offered to help me get a job. Not just that, they even drove me to work each day. They had retired anyway, but it was still nice to see them put in some effort. The job opportunity was at my High School, where I had to paint and clean classrooms. My foster Dad would drive me to the High School each day in combination with going to the only coffee shop in town. It was where he spent time with his other retired friends. For the next two summers, I worked full time at my High School.

I worked with a lot of my friends, and it was nice to earn some money. When I learned the importance of saving money, I was doing so for my first car. I sure wanted to have my own transportation as quickly as I could to escape anytime from that abusive life. I took the driver's test as soon as I was eligible and that too on my first car, which was an orange Volkswagen bug with 5-speed gears. I stalled it out at first when my Mom took me to practice driving. She offered her an automatic for my test. I was always independent and insisted on using my own car.

I was really proud to have paid for my first car. I took the test and stalled at too many stop signs and failed the first time. I didn't take any chances on the second occasion and borrowed my Mom's car. The decision was wise, and so I passed the test. I might have cleared it with my Volkswagen, too, only if I had practiced more.

My first car gave me a real sense of freedom. I couldn't wait to finish High School and live independently. I was always thinking of the future, and the profession of Nursing was always on my mind. As I approached my senior year of High School, I decided to go half-day High School and half-day vocational school for Nursing. I knew early in life that having a professional career is important. I couldn't depend on anybody else to take care of me. I love to care for others, but it doesn't mean others would want to do the same for me. Besides, I had been so used to watching over myself and my siblings that I wouldn't have wanted things any other way.

It was a very busy year that passed in a flash. I worked on weekends at a local nursing home to get a feel for working as a future nurse. I told my parents the day I graduated High School was going to be my last day at home as I will have my little car packed and be on my way. They were skeptical and weren't sure as to how I was going to do that. My High School year was very busy and goal-oriented. I had actually stopped by a recruiting office to look into joining the military and even had plans of traveling the world.

I first went into a Marine Corp office, and they suggested that the Navy was a better choice if I had plans of starting a career in medicine. I could potentially serve both in the Navy and the Marine Corps. I went next door to the Navy recruiter's office and spoke with them for a few hours. I had made my mind that I wasn't going to stay in the little town for long. I told them that I would return after I finished nursing school and took the state board exam in approximately six months. I did not share this decision with anyone.

My High School graduation was coming up while some of my serious plans and goals were yet to be fulfilled. My foster parents could not believe the goals I had set for myself.

Sometimes negative circumstances bring out the best in people and make them stronger. It did help me a great deal, making me a fighter and a go-getter. My siblings were getting nervous about my departure, and I had no idea as to whether my foster father would try to take advantage of my absence. I had to make sure my siblings were safe.

As graduation was approaching, it was time to attend the prom, but I remember my date was out of College, as he was just a little older. He was also a good distraction from an abusive household. I stayed at his house sometimes on weekends and enjoyed a happy family environment. Graduation was awesome, and I had a great time with my classmates. We were just twelve of us reflecting the size of our school. We grew up in a rural wooded area, so our after-party included a bonfire in the woods. Our beautiful long gowns were dirty by the end of the night as they were constantly dragged through the dirt. None of it really mattered. Well, we were having the time of our lives.

It was a countdown since there were literally hours before I would pack my car as promised. My car was all packed in the early hours of the morning. My foster parents got up for coffee to find me waiting to say goodbye. They were concerned about where I was going to live and what my future plans were. We had spent enough time together to not hate each other. It would have been easier for both of us if it was anything but goodbye. Goodbyes are heavy; their sound echoes until emotions are lost. It is when no matter how little the good times are, they always outweigh the bad ones, perhaps for a short period, if not forever.

I briefly explained that I had a room at the YWCA. I told them I had a full-time job and was going to study for the LVN state boards. The conversation ended with that, and I swiftly walked out of the front door to walk into a new beginning. In my mind, I had it all figured out. I followed my plans and worked the 3 to 11 pm job.

It was fun to party after work-hours with friends and sleep in until noon the next day only to start all over again. But I did not get carried away with independence and the everyday partying. My focus did not wither away from my goals but remained stagnant. I took the state boards for Nursing /LVN when the time came, and my hard work paid off. I passed with flying colors.

Chapter 4
Boot Camp

The spirit of serving my country grew firmer as I approached the beginning of a new chapter in my life. I also wanted to travel and not feel trapped in that small town. I took the ASFB test and, to no surprise, scored decently well, making me eligible to join the medical field. Finding an opportunity to work with the Marine Corps would have also served my purpose in addressing my travel endeavors. As I turned 21, by January of 1983, I found myself heading to Florida for eight weeks. My foster parents wished me luck, yet having difficulty in believing that I was actually going through with all my plans – all set to achieve my goals.

As we pulled up in buses to the Navy Base to attend boot camp, I did get a little scared to the potential uncertainty of how things were going to be. To say the least, I wasn't sure what I was to expect. We piled off the bus and stood in a straight line facing the Company Commanders (or CC's as we referred to them) that were going to mold us into good little sailors of the United States Navy!

They were shouting, getting into our faces, and to the sight, my first thought was, "*What have I done!*" We started by going to each station to get things such as uniforms, boots, and bedding for our bunk. After gathering all the essentials, we went off to the hair salon for a haircut from the top to our collars. I was kind of upset because my recruiter had told me that we could put our hair up! Later, I found out recruiters would say anything to get us to sign up!

I soon got over it, mainly because I had bigger fish to fry during those eight weeks. Of course, we marched everywhere we went, it took a minute for us to march correctly in unison. It was an open area like a High School gym where we lived and slept. I was always easy-going, so making friends wasn't difficult for me. I had learned through experience at a very early age to have each other's back at all times, and so I adopted it as a principle.

The first night was hard to sleep as you can imagine – some snored, talked, and cried through the night. If you have ever been to a military boot camp, you would know what I am talking about. Yes, we all have very different experiences, but a significant part of our lives spent at the boot camp is quite similar. The first morning at "0 dark thirty" – as they say – the CC's turned on all the lights and actually banged on the metal garbage can lids, yelling out, "Reveille!"

It scared me to death at first but got used to it after a few days. We had only 15 minutes to be dressed in PT gear and be outside to do an hour of PT, which included marching, running, pushups, and sit-ups. I was in good shape, so I did well, but I had to push a few older women in the company at the beginning as they did not have the fitness they needed. They eventually got it or got kicked out. After PT, we came in and showered, which was quite an experience. Well, I had my reasons; after all, I had never bathed with 75 women before.

I learned very quickly to take quick showers. It is something I do quite often to this day, even though it has been 30 years. We did not have much time between activities and training, so there wasn't another choice but to be organized and sufficient. We then got dressed in uniform, which at that time consisted of dungaree pants and button-down long-sleeve lighter in color material for the top, with a white undershirt underneath.

The boots were black and had to be polished every day until we could see our faces in its shine. We would march in unison to the chow hall, where the food was adequate, but I had to eat to keep up with the physical training I was about to endure. This base was co-ed, and we had our male counterparts doing their basic training. We would all be marching in the courtyards and around the base to the different areas of training. We also worked side by side when we had kitchen duty. We then marched back to the boot camp quarters. The CCs gave us the rules for the next day, such as schedules, inspections of quarters, expectations, proper wearing of uniforms, and consequences depending on the situation.

I seemed to have settled in making friends and trying to help the ones who were having a hard time being away from home. I did not miss home, as I struggled to get out of there as soon as I could. At the end of each set of bunks was an open book-shelf type piece of furniture, and in that, we had to put our inspection ready articles of clothing. As we wore them, we put clean articles that were inspection ready. Basically, there was always inspection ready articles for sudden surprise inspections.

We got each article inspection ready by putting perfect iron creases in all articles, including bras and underwear. It seemed crazy at the time, but boot camp was all about discipline and compliance. Now, I have a decent sense of humor, which is not ideal for boot camp training. During certain drills, I would get myself into some trouble with the help of some of my recruit friends who would fail to hide their giggles. It was what always got me in trouble.

On one instance, where we were all standing at attention, and to what I remember, I had my hat on backward. If you do that, you kind of look like Peter Pan! My CC approached me and got real close to my face (they were always in my personal space) and shouted real loud *"Recruit, is that how we wear our cover, you look like Peter Pan, so you need to entertain us by flying around the room!"* I was devastated, not sure how I was going to do that! I remember seeing Peter Pan, and I started to run around the room with hands up like I was flying. In the meantime, my friends are laughing, which made me laugh. Each time I laughed, another ridiculous activity was given to me.

The next activity was to do facing movements in circles for like 30 minutes. I got dizzy and was, of course, laughing. The sad or rather the funny part is that I held up the whole company during this time of silly consequences. Finally, my CC gave up, as we continued with our boot camp schedule. It seemed I did start missing home, especially my foster Mom and two sisters. I called my Mom weekly, asking, *"Can you come to get me?"* She would reply, *"Now you chose to go into the Navy, you can do it, but you do not do well with authority and discipline."* She was so surprised when I told her I was joining the military. She had a hard time believing I would even think of going into such an institution with my authority issues.

Boot camp inspections were intense at times, especially when the bed wasn't made perfectly with perfect corners. They would actually bounce a quarter on your bed, and it had to bounce. If it didn't, the CC would take all linens off the bed and throw the mattress out the window – we were two stories up. The poor recruits would usually be crying and sobbing while retrieving the mattress and dragging it up the stairs to remake that perfect bed. Fortunately, it wasn't a problem for me, courtesy the previous nursing training. I had been making beds like that for some time. I remember we would stay up all hours of the night, ironing to get the creases perfect for the next day inspection. On another occasion, I was polishing my boots that needed to shine each day. I had the shoe polish, and for some reason, I had a lighter to melt the polish, and while I did that, I accidentally put the leg of my pants on fire. It was a huge mistake. My CC threw a fit due to a safety issue, of course. Now my uniform pants were burnt on the ends, and now I didn't have uniform pants. I had to get another pair. The immediate punishment was to crawl under all the bunks to collect the dust on my uniform. As usual, I had the audience that was snickering at me once again. I did manage to keep it together at that time to avoid more punishment. Over the weeks, I passed all of my inspections and did well in classes.

As weeks of the boot camp went by, it seemed to get easier. I was looking forward to graduation and was very proud of myself to have not given up while conforming to discipline. My foster parents and two sisters did come to graduation. I had gained three stripes to Seaman due to having gone to nursing school. I marched proudly past the stands. That last weekend in Orlando, Florida, was spent at

Disney World with my family, friends; we all had a great time. Before I knew it, it was time for me to report at my first duty station. I bid farewell to my family and friends as I headed on to my next dental school adventure at the base in San Diego, CA. I was so excited to go to California all away across the country. I chose the dental school because they did not have a spot available in Corpsman school, which is equivalent to INN or Licensed Vocational Nurse. I already had attended it with High School and even had my license. I figured having some experience in the dental field might, later on, open up more opportunities for my employment.

The experience of a big city like San Diego was such an adventure, especially for someone like me coming from a small town. First of all, the living quarters during Dental School were like living in a dorm at College. All of us girls had different schedules and worked in different places. Some of us worked days while others worked nights. We had to learn who was who and respected each other's space and time. Dental school was short and sweet, but as it turned out to be, it was not my cup of tea!

While I was waiting for the next school to begin, I had planned to go home and visit my family. It seemed as though fate was waiting for me to plan on visiting my foster mother, as shortly after I finalized my plan, my foster mother had a cardiac arrest. She ended up in the Intensive Care Unit. I planned my leaves to visit her when she was able to get transferred to a regular medical-surgical floor. A few days prior to going home, I got a devastating phone call – a call I will never forget!

After receiving a message from the front desk to call home immediately, I was in a phone booth outside the barracks. My sister answered the phone, and the first thing she asked me was if I was sitting down. I couldn't make sense out of her words then. I said, *"No, I am standing in a phone booth."* She proceeded to let me know with the best words she could choose to inform me that Mom had passed away that day.

I had just spoken with her the day before, and she was so excited about my upcoming visit. She did get the chance to tell me how proud she was of me. I was going to have this visit as a healing time for us as I left right after High School, never getting the chance to spend quality time with her since I had left. I got busy with life, and as quickly time passes, I failed to adjust my visit to the home in my near future plans.

At least, I would like to believe that she never knew about the abuse from our foster father. I was devastated, and I screamed, "NO," at the top of my lungs, falling to my knees sobbing. I was screaming and kicking at the glass in the phone booth. One of my friends at the time was trying to open the door to console me. I finally calmed down, thinking how much had changed just over a day. I, no more, wanted to go home, knowing the trip home was going to be very sad. I just did not want to face it. Well, one cannot run from any reality forever.

The one person who did mean the most to me was taken away. You would think I would be used to it by now as it was a regular thing for me to have people being ripped out of my life for one reason or another. I just had another uphill battle to climb and try to make sense of it all. I took the sad journey home. I was picked up at the airport by my sister. She told me of her final days and how she was expected to recover and do well.

All the family and friends had gathered for her funeral. I remember I just wanted to leave the house, as nothing was the same without her. The house seemed empty without her presence. My foster father acted as if she was just out shopping and continued to set the table for her. As most of us know, when there is a death in the family, everyone loses control. In this situation, her own children were fighting over belongings and money. I just wanted to pay my respects and get out of there. I did feel bad, leaving my younger siblings behind who were still in High School and under the wrath of my foster father. I was in the military, and so it had to be a short visit.

I went back to my duty station in Fallon, Nevada, to wait for the next school to begin. It was rough right after my mother's death, as I felt I had nobody to report all my new adventures to. I started drinking heavily, and every night for a few months. One night we were all drinking at the dorms. I lived on the third floor, and as we were all goofing around, I fell to the ground. It was cement, but I was so intoxicated that I did not feel any pain.

An ambulance was called as many of my friends panicked. The Navy registered that as a serious alcohol issue, and I volunteered to attend an Alcohol Rehabilitation Program in Oakland, California. My first thought was how am I going to stop drinking at 21. The six-week experience was somewhat interesting. Checking into the rehabilitation center got me acquainted with people having the same issues – allowing drinking to run and ruin their life. The main objective is to get through with issues, no matter how painful they are. It is always better "coping" than "drinking."

It seems getting to those deep-rooted issues is the hardest thing ever to do. As we work through them, it does get better. It was just the beginning of my long journey of drinking and the inability to cope well. During the time I spent at rehab, I did learn that I should never drink again. I was so bad, though; I would detest Antabuse, which is a drug used to get you really sick if you drink on it. They caught on and made me swallow the pills thinking it would deter me. After about three weeks into the program, I was allowed to have weekend privileges, including day trips.

We had a chief in the group, and he invited us to a BBQ at his house. The sad part is that he served alcohol at this event. He was a higher rank and older than most of the group, and we looked up to him. He also wanted to marry me when I was 21, and he was in his forties. I thought that was very strange, and with a past of hindering sexual abuse from an older man, it definitely put my radar up.

Anyway, I went back to the rehab center, still drunk that weekend. The staff running the place just had me hushed into bed to sleep it off. As you can imagine, the last three weeks of the program were awkward with the group's older man. He said, *"I want to marry you and take care of you."* It was so creepy and still is to think about it.

During the last three weeks at rehab, I had an opportunity to do some "Drama Therapy." I bet you are wondering what it is. It is a type of therapy in which you have to act out a scenario, and pretend that a person is there whom you have wanted to say something, but cannot for multiple reasons. I was asked to do the same. In this case, it involved my mother lying in a casket and what I would have wanted to say if I had made it home before her passing.

One of the attendants of the program lay in the casket, pretending to be my mother. I started talking and relayed the message that I was sorry for acting out at times while she was trying to raise three other foster children literally up to the day she died. I also mentioned that I had wished I visited her more often out of High School until I went into boot camp, which was for 18 months.

So Corpsman school started, and I already had the

training on the outside as an LVN. It was all the same skills and information. I was able to breeze through the eight-week course while helping others succeed through the program.

Chapter 5
Starting a Family

The eight weeks of school ended, but not the friendships that I had made. Among the many new people I met was Rob. My first interaction with Rob was kind of exciting. I remember he wore a ball cap that read "'mustache rides' 25 cents." I went over to the table where four guys were sitting, all gawking at us girls. Without saying a word, I slammed a dollar on the table, and after the brief silence said, *"I will take four rides please and not all at once!"*

He looked up at me with a wide smile. As I walked away, he said to the guys at the table, *"I told you so."* I did overhear him say that but wasn't sure what he was implying to. He told me later that his friends had placed a bet on who would get my attention. Rob was a dark-haired, brown-eyed man who had sharp features. He had a very attractive smile, which was decorated with dimples.

He was a southern boy with southern charm. As you know, I am a NY girl and can be quite mouthy at times. He always liked my feistiness. So we hung out during the weeks of school and spent quality time together. When it was time to get orders for the next duty station, we both got orders to the same place miraculously. It was Corpus Christi, Texas. We could not believe how fate had paved our paths for us to stay together. Of course, we felt it was meant to be!

We both packed up and headed to Texas. The Naval Hospital was amazing, and the training we got was phenomenal. We settled into a duplex, and to be fairly honest, our financial situation was not exciting. In fact, we were quite poor at the time. He did ask me to marry him behind a beer truck! We are all wild and dumb when young. Anyway, I accepted his proposal, and we got married by the Justice of Peace. We couldn't afford a honeymoon, but that was okay, as long as we were together.

Everything throughout our relationship had happened very quickly. Things began falling apart at a similar pace. Our financial situation did not seem to improve, and neither was I able to make peace with my heavy drinking. Basically, we lacked the ability to handle situations in an adult way. After a night of drinking, he would grab me to calm me down, which I found to be domestic abuse. My past sure had an impact on me, and it showed its presence in things like these. I am never going to tolerate such behavior from anybody, especially a male. There were a few more disturbing incidences; some of them still unnerve my calmness on re-visiting my mind. On one particular day, we were in the car arguing over something unimportant. He was driving at around 70 miles an hour when suddenly, I, in my drunken state, just opened the door and jumped out on the highway. Stupid, right? I did not get hurt or get run over due to my state of drunkenness, and one might say, *"It was a good thing you were drunk!"* Well, it was one time it seemed being drunk was okay.

To speak more about our financial situation, we used to take our clothes to the laundry mat with our spare change, hoping we had enough to wash and dry the clothes. In another instance, all we had was five dollars, and believe it or not; Rob wrote the five dollars check for chewing tobacco. I was furious for obvious reasons, and so we had to eat ramen noodles until payday! The first year of our marriage ended as we received orders to 20 Palms, CA.

29 Palms, CA, is a Marine Corps base. As I mentioned earlier, I had plans to serve both Navy and Marines as a Navy Medic. The place seemed to lead to the end of the earth. By

this, I mean, one had to go through world wide training on the endless miles of the desert the military base had. My first marriage with Rob was slowly dissipating due to drinking and lack of coping with a man. I had no role models with any decent male in my life up to this time. Rob was a loving and kind southern gentleman, but I did not see that at the time. Just how some things are meant to fall in place, some things are meant to fall apart!

In the middle of this rocky relationship, my foster Dad got very ill. He was diagnosed with emphysema, which is a lung disease. He was left with only one lung, but even then continued to smoke until his last days. This is a significant part of my life, as seeing him on his deathbed was quite alarming. It was my opportunity to speak to him about my feelings and ask him the cause behind his abuse. It was also an opportunity to forgive him, as forgiveness is essential for moving on. I had to move on with my own life.

I remember approaching him at the hospital with mixed emotions of anxiety and anger, but was somewhat relieved to speak my mind finally. As I got closer, I saw a frail, pale man on a ventilator, failing to provide his body with sufficient oxygen. The first thought that came to my mind was to step on the oxygen tubing and watch him suffer as I did at the hands of his abuse for years. There were times I felt so helpless, and the wheel of time had now turned the tables. I could have done the same with him, and make him suffer for all the evil things he did to me.

I am a forgiver, and it was something I just could never have done. Anyhow, the thought last in my mind for long. I pulled up a chair next to the bed, feeling sorry for him. My foster mother had passed away a year before, and he was truly dying of a broken heart. He once told me that losing her had left him in total despair; I did believe him at that moment. I remember starting out our conversation with a positive attitude of feeling gracious to have him and my foster mother in my life. Until then, the eleven years I had spent with them were the most stable times of my life. Unfortunately, they were accompanied by some very dark moments.

I let him know he taught me to work ethics, be strong, and stick up for myself and, most of all, never take any abuse from anybody, especially a male! He proceeded to tell me that Rob had called him before we got married and asked him if he could marry me. He proceeded to ask how the short marriage at the time was going. I let him know it was rocky and that it wasn't going to last. The discussion led me to mention my thoughts about marriage, telling him that I might be married several times or not ever again. There was a battle I was fighting with my trust issues. It was something that practically started in the womb, and it wasn't going to leave me easily.

I let him know he was a role model at times and other times, of course, a nightmare for me. It was what made it tough to figure out what love and relationships really meant. I told him that I forgave him because I needed to move on with my life as I was only 22 at the time. The most important question for me was *"Why?"* He proceeded to tell me that he, too, was in foster care and was abused as a child. His words gained no sympathy as it made me feel even worse. I was like, so you wanted others to go through the pain that you did? Most people would never want that to continue and cycle into others' lives.

So I said, *"So when I have children, I continue the cycle, are you crazy?"* I remember adding, *"When I have children, I hope to be the most loving mother that I can be."* He replied in surrender, *"I am sure you will be."* I also let him know that even though I was young, I knew that abusive behavior in no form is right. The effects of it last a lifetime. My marriage was a great example of my suffering. I was not at all off to a good start in my marital life.

I then reminded him and myself that I was not going to allow my past to affect my future to the best of my ability. I committed to myself that I was surely going to use my experiences as life goes on. I remember telling him that I hated him for what he did and loved him for the good he did in my life. There were many lessons he taught me; the most essential one was learning to become a strong woman. The conversation was the last I had with my foster father, as shortly after our confrontation, he passed away. It did help me a great deal to move on with life. It was something I had been holding in my heart for a very long time, and letting go of it brought serenity in my approach.

When he passed away, my two siblings were left to fend for themselves and finish High School. I had pretty much checked out of their lives, trying to improve my own. Later on, in life, I found out they were very much affected by his abusive behavior and had been battling with their own demons.

I then returned back to my military life and rocky marriage at 29 Palm. I actually had gone to a hospital set up and military combat injury training, in case I ever had to go to the real battlefield. Although I never did, they had to prepare all of us for worst-case scenarios. The training was pretty crazy. I was in a gas chamber, which made me feel really sick. I was bleeding through the vagina, so I went into our field bathroom and passed a partial fetus. It was then I realized that I was pregnant, and had just gone through a miscarriage.

Even to this day, I'm grateful to God as he did me a favor by not testing my motherhood at a time when I sure wasn't prepared. My life was such a mess then, and it sure wasn't a good time to have a child of my own. That experience also saddened me, and Rob was also devastated that we did not know of the pregnancy. The military would not have allowed me to train due to my pregnancy, but only if any of us knew. I finished the training and returned to 29 Palms, where I had a proper D and C to prevent any infections. I did not tell anyone of that loss except Rob, and we silently grieved over it.

I continued to drink and then started to dabble into the infamous drug cocaine. I was so daring and stupid at the time as I was still active at duty and had already been to rehab once. I stayed under the radar and fortunately never got caught. The marriage eventually dissolved, and I was divorced at 22. Rob and I remained friends and were still stationed together. This was when I met Adam.

Adam, Rob, and I were all stationed together at 29 Palms, and often, we even had duties together. I worked in an OB/GYN clinic, while Adam worked in the operating room; he even assisted in delivering babies. So when I first met Adam, I saw a handsome 24-year-old man with a great smile and physique. He was from Kentucky, so it was another southern gentleman with a NY girl. He had duty in the OR a lot when we were dating, and I was out partying at times with the girls and attending events like Spring Break in the Palm Springs area. He knew that I was very outgoing, while he, on the other hand, was a bit shy. We thought we were a great match as the relationship was going to allow us to bring down some of my wildness while bringing out some of his shy-side.

We did a lot of things together too, such as road trips and seeing the countryside. Once, we even traveled to Canada to explore the Victorian Gardens, Yosemite, and other places of the beautiful country. I was on birth control, and the military life kept me occupied, so I never thought much of having children. Then in the middle of my partying days and enjoying life with Adam, I turned up pregnant. At that point, we both decided we were getting married anyway and were both very happy with the news.

I immediately quit drinking and took better care of myself. I was getting out of the military shortly, so the child wasn't going to face the difficulties of having both parents at service. So I got out and started working as an LPN and thought about getting my RN soon. I started working in the community and surrounding areas as a home health nurse, while Adam continued to work on the base. I started working with Lorna, who owned a home care agency. Lorna's entry into my life was very significant. She was my second Mom, per se.

I was about 28 weeks pregnant when I contacted a friend who worked on the base as an ultrasound tech. On my asking for it as a favor, he did an ultrasound for me. Back then, ultrasounds were few and far between unless there was a medical issue to warrant one. I will never forget this day as the results of this ultrasound is embedded in my brain. My son Kyle is my pride and joy and always will be. The tech performed the ultrasound and suddenly looked at me. I asked in surprise, *"What he has two heads?"*

He then proceeded to tell me that Kyle's kidneys were enlarged and that my amniotic fluid was low. In simpler words, Kyle was not putting out urine and may have had a blockage. Even though I was an LPN, I was devastated by the news. We went to Loma Linda hospital as we did not have a pediatric nephrologist. They felt we could wait until 26 weeks for his lungs to form completely, but we needed to see a pediatric nephrologist at Balboa Naval Hospital in San Diego every 2-3 weeks until 36 weeks.

I also went on disability at 30 weeks due to unsafe driving as my stomach hit the steering wheel and could not reach brake pedals. The visits went well, and as soon as lungs were formed, the hospital called to have me come in and get induced. As everyone loves a great birthing story, mine is interesting, to say the least.

So we checked into the OB unit to be induced on Friday evening on June 30, 1989. Balboa Naval Hospital is a teaching hospital. So Kyle having bilateral hydronephrosis, was somewhat a good learning opportunity for the students. So I settled into the hospital room and was prepped to be induced. After putting on the hospital gown, a nurse began giving the IVs. Adam settled in by my bedside to wait for any contractions.

The first 24 hours involved some contractions, and the teaching part kicked in with the physicians and their students, all taking turns checking my dilation number. I was exhausted with all the traffic, and fingers shoved up my vagina and all having a different prospection of the number. My first thought was that if I don't get an infection, it would be a miracle. On day two, Saturday, July 1, 1989, they broke my water, thinking my delivery would move along a little faster. That turned out to be the longest day of my life, with induction moving very slow. I was maybe at a 5 out of 10, so it was a long way to go!

Adam was sleeping by my side. I was in NPO, which meant all I had to survive on was ice chips, just in case I needed any anesthesia or C-Section in a hurry. I was starving, and he was eating burgers and fries! Then I remember the physician saying that one of my pelvic bones was smaller than the other, and I may need a C-section by Sunday Morning if there wasn't any progress toward the delivery. That Saturday night seemed long and slow, replicating the contractions. The next morning on July 2, 1989, at approximately 10:30 am, my pride and joy were born.

I remember them taking him to NICU to examine and determine if he needed to have an operation to check his ureter blockage. I, in the meantime, had a uterine infection as I had suspected. They had broken my water too soon, and too many fingers were inspecting me. So I was started on IV antibiotics, while Kyle was in surgery. The physician let us know that Kyle had a blockage as suspected, and it was fixed. Kyle remained in the NICU, and I got out of bed rather quickly to see my baby boy.

The first time I saw him was on my chest right after birth. The feeling of being a mother is the most special sensation in the world. I'm sure all parents reading this can relate to it. To see Kyle in the incubator with all tubes and IV lines was very scary, despite being a nurse myself. At that time, I was nobody, but a mother who was scared to death worrying about Kyle's future. The kidneys are nothing to fool around with. We were able to look at him in the incubator for the first few days, and then we got to hold him with isolation gear on as not to bring him any infections.

On the 4th of July, we wanted to see the fireworks, so I got in a WC and got on an elevator, the elevator stopped and was between floors. I had a pillow with me and had to jump into Adam's arms, and *oh did that hurt my fresh C-section incision!* We managed to see the fireworks and return to my room safely. On July 6, 1989, I was released from the hospital, but Kyle was not ready for discharge yet.

We stayed in the area and visited each day – all day, until Kyle was discharged on July 10, 1989. As a mother, I fell in love with my son more and more each day. I believe I finally figured out what it is like to love, but soon learned that the love for a child is a very different kind of love when compared to the love of a human.

The ride home from San Diego to 29 Palms was about three hours. I vividly remember that Kyle was in the backseat as per law and slept almost all the way. He started to scream to the top of his lungs, and we stopped the car, so

I could get in the back seat and breastfeed him for the rest of the ride home. I was fortunate to be able to stay home with Kyle in his first six weeks of life. Kyle also had colic the first three months, and I thought I would go crazy, trying to figure out why he cried so much; it broke my heart at the same time.

Daily, I would take walks with the jogging stroller we had gotten prior to his birth. I was a very active Mom, especially not working at the time. I struggled with his colic, and it tested my nerves and patience at times. We also went for rides in the middle of the night, so I could let Adam sleep as he still worked on the base in 29 Palms as an OR tech. The kidney issue continued, and we relocated shortly after his birth at about eight months to San Diego, where Kyle could receive close by the care with a pediatric nephrologist as those trips frequently to San Diego to 29 Palms became very difficult on all of us.

Chapter 6
Learning to be a Parent,
Learning About a Parent!

It was a challenge to relocate with a young child near the base where Adam would be working. Gladly, the military does all the work for you, including packing and then unpacking into your new home. The military also pays a housing allowance. All we had to do was find a place within the range of the given allowance. It was one less bill we had to worry about. We were in community housing and waiting for a house on the base to open. We were actually in an apartment complex, which was fairly new and in a great location. I was thinking right about then that I should look for work and think about getting back to school to get my RN.

As you can imagine finding work, going to school, and taking your young child to medical appointments frequently can be quite challenging. So before I could think of doing any of it, I had to find child care. At the time, child care was facilitated at home-settings. The hard part was that I did not know anyone and was nervous, leaving Kyle with people I did not know well. I did my homework and ran through my references and was lucky enough to find a few nice ones.

I finally landed a job at a doctor's office. I had to work a 9 to 5 shift while taking Kyle to daycare and his appointments. The frequent visits to the pediatric nephrologist included labs, ultrasound of the kidneys, and many other tests to check the urine flow. Around the age of nine months, Kyle had to have a nephrostomy tube put in to check his left kidney's daily urine flow.

I was devastated and concerned because if there was no urine flow, the kidney was to be removed. I was a young 26-year-old nurse and learned more about kidney function than I ever thought I would. At each appointment, I tried to be the mother and not the nurse. In all honesty, there were times when it was painful to have the knowledge.

I was very nervous about this nephrostomy tube, as it was impossible to find a daycare that had the knowledge and the ability to ensure the tube wasn't dislodged. We were very fortunate in this regard as our neighbor turned out to be a neonatal nurse. I went to work each day feeling comfortable that Kyle was in safe hands. As the weeks went by, unfortunately, Kyle had no urine output through the nephrostomy tube. Adam was stationed in Hawaii, so I had to deal with the situation alone. Lorna, my wonderful friend, was available for me if needed. I used to work at her home care agency. She has played a very significant role in my life, and for that, I shall forever be grateful to her. So as was expected, I took Kyle to an appointment and was told that the left kidney had to be removed since it wasn't producing any urine. In hopes that the other kidney continues to work and grow with Kyle, the doctors suggested going ahead with the procedure.

I was devastated and tried to get Adam home during this difficult time, but low and behold the military did not see a one-year-old losing a kidney a strong enough reason to bring the other parent home. I knew I could handle it as I had handled other difficult times in my life. After all, it was my child, and as a parent, I was willing to do anything for him. Deep inside, fear and concern had the best of me, but I was ready to face it with a strong attitude.

It was when Lorna's support helped me get through with Kyle's surgery. I can never forget the time I spent in the waiting room. I kept on drinking coffee, as tears continuously poured down my eyes. Lorna was my guardian angel; she still is. I wonder what would have happened to me if Lorna wasn't there. For the ones of you who don't know, the young children heal through surgeries at a fast pace and generally do well. Kyle came out of surgery, and of course, I did not recognize him as he was swollen and had tubes seemingly coming out of everywhere. Lorna was there to reassure me that everything was going to be fine.

We took turns staying all night with Kyle. In a few days, Kyle was up and playing with other children in the pediatric ward. He seemed oblivious to what had just happened and appeared to be in no pain at all. A phone call was made to his Dad, and he was given the good news of the successful surgery. However, the medical procedure was not the end but the beginning of a long journey. Kyle had to heal and survive on one kidney. At that time, I thought we could not live with one kidney, but my son proved that theory to be untrue.

We eventually moved into base housing, and Adam seemed to be gone a lot due to his deployments. Kyle had many appointments, lab work, and ultrasounds over the next few years. I finally went back to school for my RN and worked part-time as an LPN. Kyle was now going to a daycare center on base. When all my prerequisites were completed, it was time for me to apply for nursing school. My application got me on the waiting list.

Adam had told me that we were most likely to be relocated in the next year. So I had a time frame to deal with as far as getting into nursing school was concerned. I was determined to get this done. I got an appointment with the Dean at Grossmont College in La Mesa, California, to have the opportunity to plead my situation and see if I could make an impact to get in the school earlier than 2-3 years! That's the type of person I am, inserting myself in such a way to meet my goals in life.

As I sat across from the Dean explaining my situation, she asked, *"What is so special about you compared to all the others on the waiting list?"*

I said, *"Well, I am one of the few who will have the guts to make an appointment and plead my case and time frame. My spouse is currently in the military, and I have just enough time if I get in soon to complete this program. I promise you I will work hard as I understand this is a two-year program but can be completed in one year. I am already an LVN with experience and have recently finished a five-year military experience as a medic."*

She looked at me for a brief moment and then responded, *" Fair enough, you will receive a letter in the mail over the next several weeks of my decision. "* I politely left and thanked her for her time and followed up shortly with a card of appreciation, thanking her for taking the time to meet me regardless of the outcome. I felt confident, but I knew it was going to be a challenge as many others were on the waiting list. I went about my daily life and hoped for the best.

A few weeks later, I got a letter in the mail as promised. Yes, you have guessed it right, I got in! The start date was like a month away. The letter stated that if you are not there on the first day, your spot will be given to the next person. I was so excited to start the next chapter of my life. It meant having higher education, more employment opportunities, and not to mention, more income for the family. I started to plan early for my friends and neighbors to assist with daycare needs as school got closer. I had met a lot of friends and neighbors, and we all helped each other with daycare needs. It was amazing how people came together in times of need.

Military life was amazing. It is where everyone needs everyone, as all our spouses are deployed and not available at times. I am and always have been independent anyway, but the military life forces you to be even more independent. It is not only me to take care of; raising a child is a huge responsibility that I totally loved to do. It had allowed me to become a better person along the way.

The first day of Nursing school was here, and my excitement was at its peak. I woke up and got involved with my usual routine, but of course, trying to be early on this particular day. I dropped Kyle off at daycare and got on my way for school. Suddenly, I saw a car breaching the stop sign, running right into me. Before I knew it, it hit me broadside, and instantly the windows exploded, and the glass shattered. I couldn't believe what had happened. I had to get to the class, and had no time for all this! I had left early, which was the only good thing about the day!

The police and ambulance arrived on the scene. I was sitting on the curb and getting ready to call a cab because hell or high water, I had to sit in that seat to start nursing school. I am one determined person! The ambulance crew wanted me to be checked out, and I let them know I was okay and would go to ER later if needed. I explained my situation with the nursing school. I had cuts on my face and arms; glass chards were in my ski, particularly on my face.

My first thought was how was I going to walk into class like that. After realizing there was nothing that could be done, I mustered up the courage to attend school the way I appeared – bruised, and messed up. I had no choice as I had promised Adam and myself that I would not waste the opportunity. I was so distraught that at first, I told the police to look for Kyle as he may have flown out the shattered windows. They reminded me the car seat was empty, and then I realized that I had just dropped him off to daycare. What a relief that was!

My car was towed away, and I caught my cab to school. As promised, I was in the seat the first day of nursing school being stared by everyone. They all sure had learned the importance of not losing the seat. I remember people asking how long were you on the waiting list, and I had to lie against my nature, claiming to be on the list for a few years. My cuts were fresh but cleaned up for me to present myself for the first day of RN school.

My journey of that year of Nursing school was challenging, to say the least. It was late nights of studying, homework, and care plans – only another nurse can understand. Most of this year, my spouse was stationed elsewhere as Kyle, and I stayed in the area for his medical care. I took full advantage of the time to improve my life and education. The juggling of my child, work, and school was my everyday life for the next year.

The child care arrangements and scheduling of my clinical came in between 3 to 11 pm. It was hard on Kyle as he was taken to different daycare situations each week. For me to accomplish my goals, we missed out on quality time together, but he adjusted. Many people were fighting over who would take care of him, as he was loved by many. As they say, it takes a village to raise a child! I believed then, and, still, believe it to this day that all the people Kyle was exposed to and all experiences he had made him who he is today.

At the last stage of the nursing school journey, I was ready to take my state boards, and so passed the first time. The whole neighborhood had a block party to celebrate with my family and me. This is another great milestone in my life.

I had my ASN and now needed to get my BSN in the future. It was one step at a time. It surely opened doors to my future career opportunities.

Adam, shortly after my RN, got stationing orders for 29 Palms. I got a job on base as a nurse case manager for the New Parent Support Program. Basically, it was a contract with the Children's Hospital of San Diego. Kyle was at the childcare center on base for the next few years until he started Kindergarten out in the community. His medical appointments were monthly, and his one kidney had been growing with him as he continued to do well.

The job I had at the New Parent Support program was amazing. I was there for about five years working with young married military couples with young children and newborns. We also conducted parenting classes, like the daddy baby boot camp, prenatal teaching, and others. I enjoyed doing family home visits in between classes. I eventually had to work with NCIS for child abuse cases, and those types of cases really affected me as it brought my childhood memories back.

I worked long and tedious hours at times, and it started to affect my marriage, Adam felt I cared more about those families than my own. Now looking back, I did really care and spent some of my own money to make sure those children had food and even a Christmas Tree and presents. I knew my son already had everything he needed and wanted, but I had to make sure the needs of other children were not unattended.

Meeting My Biological Mother after 30 years.

Kyle was about eight at this time when I received an alarming or rather surprising phone call. One of my siblings claimed to have found my biological mother. She was in the same place the whole time, but it was us that had moved around by the foster care system. I spoke with my spouse at the time about having my biological mother out for a visit to California. It would be her first time taking a long flight from NY to California.

As a family, we agreed to it, while Kyle, only being eight years old, was trying to understand how he never knew her prior to this time. He had seen his paternal grandparents since birth but had never heard of let alone meeting his maternal grandmother. Kyle had his questions, and so I told him I would answer them later when he grew older. I only told him that not all families were the same – close and loving. I spoke with my mother on the phone, along with Barb, the other sibling I had not met. My mother apparently was living with my sister. She agreed to fly out to meet my family. I booked a flight out of Palm Springs as we lived in 29 Palms, CA, at the time. The weeks prior to the flight, I was both excited and scared. I wondered what truth the stories of my past were going to unveil. I had no pleasant memories of my early life, and neither did I hope to hear anything satisfactory.

The timeframe my mother was coming to visit was when my husband and I were to attend a Navy Ball function. My mother did stay with Kyle for an overnight. The day had arrived for me to go pick up my mother from the airport. I remember every minute of the drive to the airport. I was so nervous, after all, I had not seen her in 30 years. I parked the car at the airport, and at the time, you could go straight to where the plane landed to pick up your loved ones.

I came around the corner and could see her back to me. I only knew her by a picture that was sent earlier to me. I remember looking at her from a distance, as my eyes filled up with tears. My mind tried to find the right words to say to her but was terribly failing. I saw her in a rocking motion, and as I approached, I saw sores up and down her arms. She seemed to be scratching all over her body and sure was nervous about meeting me as well.

I walked around in front of her, and she looked up and said, *"Hi, Elizabeth!"* I replied in a weak voice, *"Hello, how was your flight?"* We gave each other a hug exchanging a few words as we both did not know what to say. We continued to say a few words as we headed to get her luggage. There had so much that had changed in the past few years. I was a parent now, and my views about her had drastically changed. Maybe they hadn't changed, but had become more empathetic; I guess that is what parenting does to you.

I spoke mostly of Kyle and my marriage, not so much about the foster care system experience, as I did not want her to feel any worse than she already did about losing her children to the foster care system. I remember her saying how she looked for us for years and never gave up and how happy she was to have that phone call from my sibling. She knew where we are were, and it brought some peace to her mind and heart.

I really wanted to focus on the present and to move forward instead of dwelling in the past. Don't get me wrong; I did want to know things about my past and verify whether my memories were true or not. It turned out as my mother let me know that some of my memories were accurate, while some she admitted she did not remember. We got to know each other a little bit during that car ride home. We pulled into the driveway, and Kyle ran out to the car to greet me as he often did. He looked at my mother, who, by the way, had no teeth at this time, and said, *"That's your Mom. She looks funny."*

Later I found out that it was due to poor dental health and drug use. It was from the mouth of a young child who let us know how he felt. My mother lived in NY all her life and had an accent that Kyle had not heard. He thought she talked funny too! I still have my NY accent to this day, but obviously not as strong as my other family members who have lived there all their lives. We made it into the house where my mother met my husband at the time. He had dinner ready as he did most of the time; he was a good cook by the way. I did not know my mother had no teeth, but fortunately, Adam had cooked some soft food, which she was able to eat.

She visited for the next two weeks and went with us to the San Diego beach. She liked the beach as it was always a few blocks from the house where she lived. It was nothing new for her except it was a Californian beach. She had never been out of NY, so flying and exploring new places was fun for her, but exhausting at the same time. I took her shopping to send her home with new luggage and some new clothes. I felt more fortunate than her at that time. I have always been a giver, and why not give to my own mother if in need.

We had a navy ball to go to and trusted my mother to stay with Kyle after we got to know her for a bit. The two of them were getting along well. They read books together and played games – Kyle enjoyed her company. We focused on getting to know her than about the past during this visit. I could see she was hurt about the past, so I wanted to show her that I did fine and not focus on the negative, hurtful feelings.

I did learn she was taking a lot of pain killers and may have been addicted. I also found addictions run in the family, and it was deep in my genetics. I don't like to use that as an excuse, but it was very obvious as my mother spoke of it on both sides of my family. I found out my Dad was an alcoholic, along with most members of his family. I continued to cook foods that she could eat and enjoy, such as mashed potatoes, lasagna, and even stuffed peppers. I cooked the peppers down to a softer texture for her.

The two weeks went by quickly, and I felt good meeting her but knew that we would never be close as time had had the best of us. I would be there for her if needed, and especially at the end of her life. After all, I am her firstborn, and so had to do what was right. I drove her back to the airport with her new luggage and new belongings, sending her home. She let me know she arrived safely, and it had been years since I saw her, but continued for several months to send money.

Later, I find out that she was using the money to get her pain pills. I was very frustrated and angry at the time, as my other sibling living with her at the time informed me of the situation. I stopped sending the money. I also stopped speaking to my mother for quite some time, but I figured I did not owe her anything. I tried to be nice to her and gave her what I thought would be money spent on other things of need. I was not contributing to her pain pill habit.

My life continued as I was involved in my job while working and taking care of my family. Over the next two years, my husband and I started to drift apart, wanting different things in life. I tried to spice up the marriage by going out with other couples and trying to do more things besides him and Kyle playing video games with each other in different rooms! That was fun for them, but not me.

As everyone knows, if life does not change at home, you go elsewhere to find fun. I was going through, as they say, mid-life crises. I was 36 years old at that time. At the time, my husband looked it up and said to me, *"It says men go through this, not women."* I replied, "Well, the unhappy one goes through it. We even renewed our vows at the 10-year mark and invited all our close friends to celebrate at a nearby bed and breakfast place. The friends included Lorna and John, and couples we have had as friends over the years meant the world to us.

We went to see a therapist, and she told my husband that I never had a chance to have fun as a child, I grew up quickly at no choice, and now I want to have that fun. According to her, he had two choices, go out with me, and have fun together or let me go. Kudos to my husband, as he decided to try to go out with me and try my craziness. We worked on our social life doing things such as dancing and taking line dance lessons, live music, and drinking. It only took him a few times out, and he realized it was not for him. I sort of married my opposite, a quiet low key guy, while I was a social butterfly who loved to be out. Eventually, we had our clashes, and things seemed to progress for the worse.

The thing was that even our married friends were mellow. I had a hard time finding friends to share that lifestyle. I had not drunk or partied much for the first eight years of Kyle's life, as I was trying to be that great mother and wife. Happiness is very important to me. Those ten years of marriage were fabulous and fulfilling.

I learned a lot of what love is with my husband and his close family, but when you grow up in the kind of environment I did, you have periods of feeling smothered with love and need your space and time. It may sound weird to some, and neither am I proud to say this, but I cheated outside the marriage and got attention elsewhere. Such situations do not allow the relationship to last, but at the time, serves its purpose.

Chapter 7
Tennessee, California and the "Premonition"

The day we sat Kyle down to let him know that we were not going to live together anymore was one of the toughest days of my life. The thing that made it less painful is that my husband, at the time, did most of the talking and explained to Kyle that it was not his fault. He told him that we would both be there for him at all times; we would live close to each other so he could be with whoever and whenever he wanted.

I remember Kyle vividly saying. *"But we are the three musketeers and always supposed to be together."* It broke my heart, but the decision had already been made. My husband had decided he was going to let me go and be happy. To this day, we are still friends and always will be; he is a good man. He deserved to have the kind of person he was looking; he deserved to be happy.

Since I decided to leave, it was only fair that my husband and Kyle stayed in the house we bought. I was the one who had to move out. I initially moved in with the guy I had been seeing, and at the beginning, Kyle stayed with us. To what it seemed, I think he was a little confused. The situation did not last for long as Kyle and I eventually moved into a new place where it was just us.

He loved living that way – just him and I. I eventually got another RN job in the next town. Since it was a 12 hour night shift, Kyle stayed with my ex for three days in a week and with me when I had my days off. Kyle adjusted well and even felt that he got more spoiled due to our separation. I always rented a home too big for the two of us but loved the space. Kyle loved it too; after all, he could comfortably have his friends over.

In one of the homes we rented, I made some friends next door. She was a single Mom with two young girls. She also had a boyfriend. We clicked since the moment we met. Often we had BBQs together, and when Kyle was over, he would spend time with the girls. We all would even eat together at times.

Kyle's Dad lived with a couple of other military friends as we sold the house shortly after the separation. It was good for Kyle to stay there as the guys taught Kyle to do his own laundry and fulfill other such responsibilities of a young man. Kyle also grew up with a German Shepard who went wherever Kyle went, so we also shared the German Shepard, Mia.

One day I decided to move closer to a friend of Kyle's. It was a house on a corner across from where Kyle's best friend lived. It had a big front yard where I could trim the roses and the fruit trees. The house had three bedrooms and two bathrooms. It also had a good size garage where I eventually put a ping pong table. Kyle became the ping pong champion when friends came over. We had a lot of BBQs there.

Kyle and I played a lot of ping pong, and well, my little champ beat me most of the time. The backyard had a pool that needed to be fixed up and relined. I decided to ask the landlord if I could fix up the pool and take some money off the rent. Gladly, the landlord agreed. To achieve this goal, I invited friends for help. A group of friends and I relined the pool and fixed the deck by rebuilding it and painting it. We then filled the pool with water and bought all the chemicals to keep it up.

The pool and house were used a lot over the next few years, as lots of friends visited, and lots of gatherings were held here. I continued to work nights; Mia spent more time with me than she did at Adam's. One evening she figured out how to lift the latch on the fence and get out. She roamed in the neighborhood and then let herself back in before I got home in the morning. She was one smart German Shepard!

I found this out later, of course, from the neighbors one night, she went through the garbage cans and tossed up the neighborhood with trash everywhere. One particular morning, the pound truck was looking for a German Shepard that had been reported seen in the neighborhood going through trash cans that were out for pick up. They just happened to stop me and asked as I pulled into the neighborhood that morning after work. I was devastated as I knew it was Mia. I said, *"I will let you know if I see her."*

I was like frantically driving around the neighborhood looking for her. There she was in the neighbor's yard visiting while she watered her roses. I yelled out the window to get home now. I got her in the yard just as the pound truck drove by slowly. At that moment, I rigged the latch, and she never got out again to trash the neighborhood.

Well, I thought she would always be with us anyway. There was a time when she disappeared for about two weeks. Kyle and I looked for her everywhere, including through the desert terrain. We even thought the coyotes had gotten her. We put a picture of her in the nearby pond and the veterinary office. It turned out that someone had brought her to the vet and we got an address to find her. This dog was part of our family and Kyle's best friend since he did not have any siblings.

I remember knocking on the door and hearing Mia bark. Kyle was so excited to have finally found her. The woman of the house opened the door. As we called Mia, the woman said, *"My kids love this dog."* I replied, *"This dog has been in our family since she was six weeks old, and she is ours."* They reluctantly gave her back to us. Now our family was complete again. It was a long two weeks looking for her. In a way, Mia always kept us busy.

The guy I saw during the marriage was in and out of my life at different times. I actually had to get a restraining order against him as he continued to stalk me around town. At around the same time, Kyle's Dad went on a deployment, and while my Mom was having a hard time with the situation. In the best interest of my family, I decided to relocate to Tennessee during that year to support her. The town of 29 Palms had nothing to offer to me except many good and bad memories.

After moving to Tennessee, the first thing I did was enroll Kyle in a school. He was a good student through and through. He had done well in school over the years receiving awards for his excellent academic results. It's not that he wasn't affected by the divorce, but he coped up really well with the situation. My husband's family has always been special to me and still is to this very day. His Mom is very special to me, and so does Kyle adore her.

Anyhow, after settling in, I started looking for a job as a nurse. I found a position as a Director of Nursing at a Nursing Home, which was about 30 minutes away from home. Kyle was busy getting to know his cousins and settling into a routine. The house was a neat two-story, which looked like a barn from the outside. It was in the middle of a small wooded area. I stayed on the second floor in the loft; it was very cozy and comfortable.

I settled into my new position and enjoyed spending time with my ex's family. During that year, the guy started to talk with me again. In all honesty, against my judgment at the time, I started to miss him. 29 Palms wasn't all I left, as I did leave great friends behind.

There was a facility dog named Belle. She was a Golden Retriever that had grown very fond of me. I ended up bringing her home, and so we had two dogs at the house, Mia and Belle. Around the same time, my ex returned home from deployment. We tried to see if we could re-connect and even took a brief trip to Las Vegas.

On this particular trip, I showed how my wild side was really coming out with drinking and dancing at the bar at Coyote Ugly in Las Vegas. I puked on the plane most of the ride back, and we decided to get back together was something that wasn't going to happen. I decided to go back to California. I did get the opportunity to take Belle the golden retriever with me, and she was my rock for a while. We did everything together. Kyle did stay in Tennessee with his grandmother as I was still trying to figure out where I wanted to live and who I wanted to be with.

As I drove back to California and had left my child for the first time ever, he was about 13 years old. He was with his grandmother and his father. I felt like a bad mother, although I let my son know that I would come back and get him once I got myself into a more stable position. I got back to California and started seeing the wrong guy again. I also went back to my job as an RN supervisor for a 99-bed facility, where I used to work nights.

I started working nights again and working with my current nurse friends. Some of these friends were from the military. I had a great friend, Julie. She had married to Mark, a former Marine, and thought she could not have children. She was only married a few years and had two little girls back to back.

We hung out together on weekends, doing BBQs and horseback riding on her ranch home in 29 Palms. I would watch her children at times; the elder ones were eight and ten-years-old. Mark also had a 13-year-old, so it was five children altogether. Also often she rode motorcycles with her friends. I was backdating the older guy again.

We continued to work together and see each other on weekends as my guy friend worked Thursday to Sunday at the prison. He was a prison guard or a correctional officer, as they say these days. One night we were at work, and she started to tell me about a premonition. At around 3 am, as we worked nights, she and Mark had a day planned on a Saturday to go on a motorcycle ride Palm Springs, CA.

She had asked me if I could watch the kids that day while they went on the motorcycle ride. I told her I would love to like always. After the motorcycle ride, we had plans to have a BBQ later in the evening. It was something we often did. We were discussing her plans for the motorcycle ride, and she started to tell me that she had a strong premonition that she would get into an accident on the way home. She told me her premonition in great detail.

My first immediate reaction was suggesting her not to go this weekend. She insisted that Mark was really looking forward to the Palm Springs bike rally, and they had planned it for a long time. I was intrigued by the rest of the premonition. Until then, I had not met anyone who had told me about a premonition before. So she goes to the rally; they have a great time until they are a mile distant from home. They get hit!

The impact was so intense that she flew over the bike and hit the hood of a car. They are both in a coma for some time. Julie couldn't battle her way out of the coma and passed away. Mark was lucky enough to survive. She had even told me that she had taken a 500,000 life insurance policy. She wanted me to take care of Mark and the kids, at least until the grieving settled. She thought Mark and I would be good together.

I was friends with her before she had gotten married, which lasted for two short years, as the accident consumed her life. I was in shock at listening to her revelation. We are both really tired, and so I asked her, *"Are you sure this wasn't a dream you had?"* I wanted her to cancel the trip, as I was scared of hearing the details and taking out the life insurance.

"Do you want to die?" I asked in outrage. *"You have five children and a husband that needs you."*

She was so in love with her Mark that she decided to go anyway. Over the two weeks before the motorcycle trip, we had talked several times, and she was still insistent on going. I could not change her mind. I also did not let anyone know as I thought at the time, or rather hoped that they would return safely. As the day of the trip arrived, I got up early to get over to her house to watch the children. The morning was chaotic as everyone was rushing around, getting ready. When I walked in, children were crying, and she was arguing with her teenager.

I will never forget what the teenager said, *"I hate you, and I hope you die on the way home!"* I freaked out and asked the teenager to apologize to her mother. I said, *"She loves you so much, and you did not mean that!"* The teenager never apologized, as she was too angry at the time. They proceeded to leave for the day trip to Palm Springs. I got the children ready, and we went to the park to blow off some steam as having five children in the home could get chaotic.

We went home to have lunch and took some food out for the BBQ that we were supposed to have when they returned home. It was an October evening in 2003. I did receive a call, Julie, a few times that day to check on the kids. She even told me that she would be leaving for home at around 5 pm. The time we had scheduled for the BBQ was around 6:30 pm. I anticipated their return but was getting a little nervous as the clock struck past 7. It was getting a little late, and since they were traveling, I did not expect them to answer their phones, so I didn't call. I waited patiently and nervously.

At around 9 pm, the police came up the drive, and I knew why they were here; I panicked immediately. The younger children were already in bed. The boys and teenagers were still awake and waiting for their parents to return. Obviously, the BBQ did not happen, and we all ate dinner earlier. I answered the door and was told that there had been an accident. They were both rushed to the hospital.

I don't know if anyone could see how I felt from the inside and just collapsed at the door. I did not even have a clue as to how I would get hold of their family as they were both in a coma. The teenager had the number to her Mother and Grandmother, so we called the family and let them know. Breaking the news to them wasn't easy. We told them that they were both hospitalized and in a coma as it was all the information we had.

I had all five children and needed to reach out to friends to help me assist with the children as the situation unfolded. I could not and did not go to the hospital until their family arrived from Maine and New Hampshire, which was where my friends were originally from. As family and friends started to gather at the house to assist with the children, I was able to get to the hospital and see what exactly happened.

I remember being so nervous and anxious as I entered the hospital to the ICU where they both were. A friend of mine had gone on the ride and witnessed the accident. They were hit on the bike from the side by an 18-year-old driver who was still not at the legal age to drink. The teenager was returning from his first keg party and was obviously drunk. He went through a stop sign, and as a result, took an innocent life. I knew that I had returned back to California for a reason. Back then, it was just very difficult to understand.

I had to speak to somebody about their injuries and to have some idea of the future held. The husband had flown off the bike and landed on the hood of the car. He broke every bone in his face, also breaking his hips. My friend had flown off the front of the bike and landed on the pavement. They both had all gear on, but she had a head injury and swelling on the brain.

They were in the hospital for about two days, as their friends, including me, were caring for the children. The parents had arrived to relieve us or take turns going to the hospital and caring for the children. The little girls of twenty months and nine months were not as aware of the parents not being there. As you can imagine, the older siblings were very worried and concerned, especially the teenager who was upset with her mother the morning she was leaving.

It seemed like forever, but finally, after about five days, the husband woke up. His jaw was wired and shut due to the face bones he had broken. He also lost an eye. My friend has not woken up yet at this time, and we were all worried. We focused on Mark as we were excited to see him awake, but knew he had a long recovery period ahead. A few more days passed, and we were told that Julie had a brain injury with too much brain damage. They told us that even if she woke up, she would most likely have no brain activity and no quality of life.

I had worked in a sub-acute unit with patients with brain injuries, and we had promised each other never to let the other be living like that. Mark knew that too. At this point, her family and husband had to make a hard choice of letting her go. I remember feeling devastated by her premonition coming true. The accident happened as she had described, and I started feeling guilty that I did not share it with anyone, even though she did not want me to. She only wanted me to take care of her family during the grieving process.

Following the days of her demise, Mark started his long journey of recovery as we, her friends, planned for her funeral. One of the hardest days of my life had appeared before me, having to sit the children down and tell them that their mother was never coming home. The boys were devastated, and so was everyone else. The husband had to plan the funeral from his hospital bed as he could not attend due to his injuries. I remember he had a lot of milkshakes and soft food during the time of his wired jaw.

Her family came out to California for a funeral and to transport her body back to New Hampshire. The funeral was a closed casket due to her injuries, and it was a good thing as we wanted the children to remember her the way they had seen her the morning she left for Palm Springs. She hugged each child on her way out and let each one know how much she loved them.

She had to deal with the teenager's arguments and harsh words the day she left. We had the service on Halloween night, and Mark had a speech prepared, which was read by the family. Her body was then sent home with her family. Mark's extended family started to each take a child or two back to Maine to their homes as Mark recovered back in California.

I, along with my other friends, stepped up to help Mark with the recovery and the grieving process. The couple's extended family was very grateful for the friendships the two of them had. They thanked us for caring for the children during this difficult time. It seemed natural for me to step up and assist as needed, as I did the exact same thing with my siblings, years ago.

Chapter 8
Everything Happens for A Reason!

I had not stopped seeing the guy, so I was taking turns with friends to care for Mark with his recovery as he went through physical therapy. He finally was able to go home to recover in between appointments. It was when I was able to share the premonition information with him. It turned out he thought it was going to happen either way. He said that it was in the cards for our lives to deal with the difficult situation. He said that everything happens for a reason.

I felt less guilty as we went through this together. I felt good, at least about fulfilling her wishes and dealing with the grief process together as she wanted us to do. We did not do a good job at first, as we both dealt with it by emptying many bottles of whiskey. At the time, I guess that was our preferred coping mechanism. We spoke of her frequently for a long time, laughing and crying almost every day.

Just as my friend had predicted, we got closer, but I had another life, and so had to get back to my plans. For a while,

I went back and forth with my guy friend to the life of my other guy friend. I was very torn and confused with the situation getting kind of out of hand. I was living now in Arizona and would visit my friend in California on weekends as he continued to recover.

He spoke of the half-million dollars he got for the life insurance. Neither one of us had ever had that kind of money, so it was indeed overwhelming. He bought a new vehicle to haul all the children he now had to raise alone. We discussed when he went to Maine; I would come to visit, but made no plans of staying. We finally, after months of therapy, separated. He went to Maine to reunite with his family, and I went back to my life of travel nursing, and to Arizona with my other guy friend. I was in touch with him the whole time, though; we frequently talked as he let me know how the kids and he was doing.

I went on with my life, dealing with one day at a time. As always, my guy friend worked from Thursday to Sunday at the prison in California. I worked in Arizona per diem at an agency while also working at the prison system in Arizona. It was for a brief period. I worked per diem so I could have a more flexible schedule to work, getting to choose when and where I wanted to work. This particular week I went into my agency office to get my shifts for the weekend, and my recruiter at the time, a guy little younger than myself, asked me if I would join him for Mexico for the weekend.

I was like, why not?! It sounded like fun, and my relationship was on the rocks anyway. My gypsy soul was not sure where I was headed. I took the opportunity to have some fun after that journey with my girlfriend's death. It had been a while since I had taken a vacation, and there couldn't have been a better time. So on Friday afternoon, my recruiter picked me up from near my home, which was in the Phoenix area at the time, since I resided with my older guy friend and his mother. We headed down the highway for Mexico via Phoenix way, and as soon as we hit the border, we could drink alcohol in the car. I know it was not the smartest idea, but it was legal.

We arrived in Mexico when it was dark and checked into the hotel, after which we went to find something to eat. We found a place that looked popular with the number of people that were there. The music playing made the place look happening. The next day we hit the beach and the sun, drinking margaritas, enjoying the sea breeze. It was lots and lots of day drinking. In the evening, we were still in our swimwear and got into a cool bar with music playing. The evening turned into the night, and it was time for some self-exploration.

My friend and I separated to meet other people, something I am always up for doing. My personality has always been at ease to meet new people at any given time and place. These particular people were all from Phoenix, as we were close to that area. It was fortunate that I got to know them because, as it was closing time, my friend was nowhere to be found. It was so dark outside, and I really could not remember the name of the hotel we were in! It's not easy to remember anything after uncountable rounds of drinks, let alone the hotel's name.

The four gentlemen I met drove me around to see if they could safely get me to my hotel. They all came together as one of them owned a three-story condo on the beach, who made a guy's trip annually. Of course, I picked them out of the crowd. I always get a gut feeling about people, something that tends to happen when you do as much traveling as I do. These guys made me feel totally safe. I could not pick out the hotel in the dark, and my new friends refused to let me roam around as it was unsafe out there. Mexico was unfamiliar territory for me, so they decided to take me to the three-story condo to get some sleep.

We had planned to find my hotel and friend in the morning. It was that time of my life when I came across true gentlemen. It hasn't happened quite often with me. The only clothes I had were a bikini, which I wore all day and night. One of the guys let me wear his t-shirt and boxers! I had offers from all four to borrow clothes to wear to bed. It was when I find out who all four of them are. The first one was a white guy who owned the condo. He was about 55 years of age; he was single and good looking. I was around 40 years old at the time. The second guy was black and about 45, the third guy was white and about 65. He seemed very old to me back then, so he was! The fourth guy was white and 28 years of age. He was the only married one in the lot.

I had three stories in the condo to choose from amongst the many bedrooms that were there. The married one wanted me to snuggle and sleep next to him. I let him know that I do not mess around with married men. I may have done some not so good things and made not so good decisions, but ruining anybody's marriage was never going to be my choice. He was disappointed but understood. I slept on the third floor in a spare bedroom alone as planned.

The next morning I woke up and heard voices on the outside deck facing the ocean. The guys were having coffee. It was the first time we all had time to talk without loud music in the background. They wanted to know more about me as one of them asked, *"What is your story?"* I told them there is not enough time for them to know my story! I did tell them I was living in the Phoenix area with an older guy and not sure how long it would last. The owner said if anything happened, I should let him know as he would take care of me.

At the time and still, to this day, I do not need anyone to take care of me, and I let him know that but thanked him for his kindness. To this day, though, I do know he meant it, and I would have had a wholly different outcome to my life, but it was not meant to be as I look back. Men being boys, the subject of who I would sleep with in the group came into discussion. I looked at each one and said, the young and old one is out for obvious reasons due to age and marital status. The oldest guy surprised me by saying, *"I just want to watch."*

I was taken aback by that statement as I had never had anybody say that in my life. It just seemed wrong! For everyone reading this book, the next few paragraphs may or may not shock you. I did do the owner in the shower as the other guys had their ear to the door – admitting later. I needed a shower anyway. I also did my first black guy who was too big, but gentle and found out later the older guy snuck in the room and watched from the corner.

The married guy harassed me all weekend, and I gave him a little make out time, and well, he was happy with that. Anyway, we finally left the condo and went to find my friend and hotel. This was a three day weekend, and we were now on day three. I finally recognized the hotel we checked into, and as we walked in the lobby, entered the elevator, where he was. He was so excited to see me and said, *"I thought somebody killed you and dumped your body."* I was like these guys right here looked out for me, so there was nothing to worry about.

We all continued to enjoy the beach and margaritas. Before I knew it, it was dark, and I realized I was not going to get home earlier than my guy friend. I felt trouble coming. At that time, I figured that since I was already late, there was no point in rushing. I was going to be in trouble no matter what. We stayed and continued to drink into the night with our new friends. We finally said goodbye and got on the road after thanking my new friends for their hospitality.

On the way home, I spoke with my recruiter friend and let him know that things were going to get messed up. I told him that I was probably going to move on after this week and so needed more shifts from his agency. I told him that I would pick up my last check at the end of the week. He understood and dropped me off with my suitcase a block before the house.

As I was wheeling my suitcase to get to the door, my heart rate increased as it was practically beating out of my chest. What saved my nerves was that I was still kind of drunk from all the drinking I had done over the last three days. I went up to the door, and it was locked, so I had to ring the bell. As I stood there waiting, I was deciding whether or not I needed to tell the truth and face the consequences of him being angry. He opened the door and stated, *"How was work?"*

I looked at him and said, *"Does it look like I went to work?"* After all, I had a suitcase, and tan like I had been at the beach for several days. I went upstairs to put my clothes in the laundry from the weekend and take a shower. I then went downstairs, where he was having a drink and trying to figure out where I went. I walked into the living room and sat down to explain where I was. I told him I went to Mexico for the weekend instead of working.

I also told him that I had gotten invited by friends last minute, which wasn't entirely wrong. He looked angry and did not say a word. I decided I would sleep in the spare room that night because I already knew I was leaving at the end of the week and did not want to get into any kind of pointless argument. I was still a little buzzed from the drinking and was settling in to fall asleep. Suddenly he barged in the door and jumped on the bed, straddling me and grabbing my neck. He said, "I can break your neck in one snap."

I was terrified but somewhat in control. I told him that if he broke my neck, he needed to break his mother's neck, eventually landing on the other side of the bars. He was a correctional officer at the prison, so he knew what it was like to be there. Now that I think back, it reminded me of my foster father and his thought of control over me. He did not know what to say or do after that statement. He finally decided to yell at me, call me names, and throw me around the room. He was over six feet and very strong, so there was no way I could stop him from being despicable.

He also was able to punch me in the face a few times during this whole altercation. I was laughing at him, letting him know, which he had forgotten that if any man touched me, I never stayed. He was like, *"You have no place to go."* He finally left the room and went to sleep after all the adrenalin wore off. The next morning when I looked at the mirror, I was pretty sore. I saw the bruising on my face and body. I remember going downstairs to get some coffee and found his mother awake. I still remember her words. *"I did not teach my son to act that way towards anyone, especially women. I am so sorry."*

I let her know that I was not going to turn him in because she was there. I said, *"I would never take him away from you. I will leave quietly when he returns to work at the end of the week."* She agreed to that plan and even offered to assist me with the packing. He finally came downstairs and had the audacity to say, *"You need to get back to work."* I replied, *"Yeah. Looking this way sounds like a good idea, not!"* I let him know I needed to heal and will return after the bruises had faded to some degree. I acted as if nothing happened and went on with our week.

We did BBQ, and he made me my favorite homemade pina colada's. We carried on as if nothing had happened. He did apologize a few days later, and I accepted it. He honestly had no clue I was leaving, and I kept it that way, so there was no further arguing or fighting. The end of the week slowly arrived. I had done all the planning in my head as to how I was going to disappear. My friend's husband wanted me to come to visit Maine, and he sent me an airplane ticket. I acted as if nothing is changing and said goodbye to him on that Thursday morning as he went off to work.

He mentioned that he hoped I would go to work on the weekend. I did not really respond to that comment. He pulled out of the driveway and started immediately packing as most people who know me know, when my mind is made up, there is nothing that can change it. His mother helped me pack. I hugged her and told thanked her for everything. I hoped my escape would not make him take out his frustration on her. I took his second car to a nearby bar and got something to eat as I had several hours to go before my flight. I also had no plan for who was going to take me to the airport. I hoped to meet someone at the bar to take me.

I frequently lived on the edge with no particular plan. It is who I am, and well, there is nothing I can do about that. It turned out I met several people, including a cop off duty. I told him my story and why I was leaving. He agreed to follow me to my friend's house to drop his car off and take me to the airport. The cop said he would look out for his name in the future, for if he ever hurt anyone again, he sure would be punished. I did not want to turn him in, but I also was hoping he would never hurt anyone again.

I was dropped off to the airport and never looked back. I knew he would be upset when he got home three days later to find me gone. I did leave him a letter explaining why I left, telling him to make no attempts to locate me. I flew into Maine for a visit to Mark, as I promised a few months ago. I landed in Maine and felt safe with Mark. He knew of the incident and wanted to go after him. I let him know he was not worth it and that I was never going to see him again. He was settling into his new home and had put the girls in daycare. I surprised them and went to pick them up. They lived in a small town, Gray Maine, and this daycare was a small homemade into a daycare.

I remember going in to get the girls. They were so dirty as their faces had dried up food all over. I let Mark know that we needed to find a nicer daycare and that the girls deserved better. He admitted it was all new to him, and without a woman in his life, he was doing the best he could. I assured him I would help with finding a new daycare. I found a daycare close by the home Mark had bought that his brother had built for him. His family was into building homes and selling homes. The home was a two-story at the time that had a nice basement with living space.

I visited for a few weeks and got to see the camp on the lake that Mark's brother owned. It was more like a mansion, two-story, and many rooms for the whole family to stay on occasion – it was a summer home. I went on this particular visit and spent time with Mark and the kids on the lake. The place had a boat and wave-runners for the adults and children to enjoy. There was even a trampoline in the middle of the lake to jump on and dive into the water. I was starting to realize how much work it was to have all those kids at different ages and stages of life. The young toddlers were cranky and having crying fits, the boys were acting out, and the teenager was mad at life as teenagers are. During that visit, I told Mark that I was not sure about being able to handle all the kids as I was raising one, which was my only plan in life. As we all know that life changes in a minute. I just could not promise a life with him at that time.

I left Maine and went back to California to stay with my friends Bonnie and Yancy. They were my friends from the military whom I had known for many years. I knew them even before my son Kyle was born. I stayed with them and worked nights at a local hospital. I stayed in touch with Mark just about every day. I struggled with money, and he wired about 10,000 dollars to my account, hoping that I would visit soon. At the time, I started to miss Mark and the kids and my own son Kyle, who continued to go to the Bahamas with a friend's family. I missed him so much and needed to get it together soon.

I only lasted about 2-3 months and finally went back to Maine for a visit with Mark and the kids. The visit included seeing his extended family – siblings, and parents. I was growing fond of the whole family. For the first time in my life, I took about six months off work. Mark and I just had fun getting to know each other. After all, we had the life insurance money. We would take the kids to daycare and just go to brunches, lunches, and drinking in and out of the home. Now looking back, it seemed to be our way of coping with Julie's death.

The girls were getting older, and we told them about their Mom and showed many pictures and videos. The home had several pictures of her, as we did not want the children to forget about her. Mark's parents were fond of me and thought we were drinking too much, especially for someone who was responsible for raising small children. We had several conversations about our coping strategies. His mother felt it was not in the children's best interest and that we needed to get a better handle on it. She said she was going to take the children until we straightened up.

The boys were acting out in school, and the teenager was going through a period of depression and cutting. Also, the boys' father wanted custody of them. Eventually, the boys moved to New Hampshire with their father and Julie's extended family. This is where Mark and I only knew we only had the three girls now, but believe me, we put up a fight for those boys. Unfortunately, or not, their biological father won. It was hard on the other children as they missed their brothers. We decided I would stay and would drive to

Tennessee and get Kyle to join the family. Kyle was aware of the situation as he knew Mark and Julie. Kyle was now about 15 years of age and wanted to come live with Mark and me.

I let Kyle's grandmother know that we were coming to get Kyle, and he needed to pack his things. We drove out as a family to get Kyle. It was a road trip, and I was so excited to get my precious son. He and I were going to be together again. He did well with his grandmother and was ready to go on another adventure with his mother.

Chapter 9
Can't Stop Being Myself!

The road trip back was fun, and Kyle bonded with the girls nicely. His sense of humor made them laugh often, and it was not long before they began considering Kyle as their elder brother. The teenager felt she had a big brother too, and they both went to High School together. Kyle is an only child who seemed to be loving the big family he then had. In the gist of all, we finally made it from Tennessee to Maine.

We enrolled Kyle into the local High School. It was a very small school, but Kyle prefers small towns to big cities as he grew up in small towns. The teenager looked up to Kyle as a big brother at home and school, indicting that she always wanted a brother. We had all started to blend as a family. I got a job as a nurse unit manager at a nearby Alzheimer's locked unit. My shift was from Monday to Friday, having all weekends and holidays off. Mark picked up a job at the geek squad at Best Buy; he was great with electronics. The daycare center nearby that the girls went to was working out great.

Mark would send me flowers frequently to my workplace, and all my friends would speak of his sweetness. We frequently had a conversation about how long I would be staying. I would just say that we shall let time decide. I always reminded him that I wasn't sure if things could be the way they were, forever; he understood.

As days and nights were taking turns, we were enjoying each other's company. We had bought a boat, RV and jet skis with my favorite color purple; my name was engraved on it! Mark would surprise me with new things frequently. One day, I reminded him that we need to invest some of that money for the kids for college, as Julie had discussed with me. Before making the investments, we decided to add a third level to the house over the garage.

It was to make a fun atmosphere for the kids as well as for us, the adults. It turned out to be awesome as we included a big-screen TV, pool table, a small bar, darts, and a jukebox. It was truly a place away from everyday life, and often after the kids were in bed, Mark and I went up there either alone or along with our family and friends. The place kept us away from the bars as much as we liked it too.

We still seemed to continue to drink heavily, and Mark would even go up there alone to do his own grieving as it was still fresh to us even after a few years. On a couple of occasions, I remember that after he went up there all of a sudden, I heard him yelling, cursing, and throwing things. The pain was overwhelming at times. I would just leave him alone, allowing him to exhale out his agony. He felt at times that it was not fair that she died and left him with the kids to raise alone. His concerns were on point, as he did not do well alone.

The kids continued to grow and develop their personalities. The tantrums continued as they were toddlers and teenagers. I was thinking at the time, so I let Mark know that I had not signed up for this drama. Kyle and the teenager helped with the little ones when Mark and I needed a break. Looking back, I think we took them for granted and should have done a better job. We both were still on the whiskey and emptied a bottle quite frequently. The kids saw this but didn't say much. I feel bad about how we acted at the time.

We took the teenager to an inpatient psychiatric unit to deal with her grieving issues. She instead, was focused on how cute the boys were there. It was hard to get her to focus.

She also liked her new brother Kyle, and we had to speak to her about that! She would often come out half-dressed, and her father would have to tell her to go put more clothes on! There was a time where she thought I liked Kyle more because he did well and behaved himself. He even helped her with her homework, but I let her know I loved them both.

At one point, she did not want to follow the house rules and tired of her reluctance; Mark decided to send her back to her mother's for a while. She then begged us to come back, realizing that we were not so bad after all and that she was better off in our household. When she came back home, she gladly followed the rules, and so was doing well.

The time had come to make the investment for the future of the kids. Mark agreed to put half the money of about 250,000. He even bought me a new vehicle outright and just wrote a check. Time was flying by, and before I knew it, Mark asked me to marry him. It was about in 2005. I hesitated at first and let him know once again that I did not know how long I would stay. He said he was okay with that, and after numerous discussions, we ended up getting married on 5/5/2005. The wedding was held at Cinco De Mayo, and of course, it involved lots of alcohol. This was a fabulous wedding on the beach in Maine with a sand dollar wedding cake, limo, and DJ. I remember my sister coming and asking me if this is what I wanted, and I told her what I had discussed with Mark, *"Not totally sure about how long I would stay."*

Not long after the wedding, I wanted to go out with girlfriends to the bars again. I met a friend Sonya at work who was the only one who wanted to have drinks after work and on some weekends. Mark and I went to the local bars, and I would often not be ready to go home. He would say okay and that he would come to get me later when I thought I was ready. As with my other marriage to Kyle's Dad, I started the same pattern of not wanting to be home and have my own life. It is a very bad place to be in my own head. I have this perfect life in front of me with money, love, and family, and I don't know what to do with it. I should embrace it, but I don't know how too, except for short periods.

It was very frustrating, and I knew I was going to hurt a lot of people again, including my own son Kyle! As we know, alcohol makes us selfish as it had made me many times over and over in my life. I continued to drink with and without Mark. Things were falling apart until one particular incident hammered the last nail in the coffin. Kyle came to the beach to pick me up after many hours of drinking, and I got kicked out of a bar on the beach after lap dancing many guys in my bikini – not proud of that today. My son had to see me that way, what a mess I was!

Kyle took me home, and Mark and I discussed how I was getting out of hand the next day. This was approximately a year after the wedding, and I decided I better get out before the kids got too attached as they already had started calling me Mom. I believe this brought me back to my childhood, where I was acting like my mother, who had given us away, except, of course, they were with their Dad. I had to let them go early in life, so they had plenty of time to get a real mother in their life.

I often thought of how my friend Julie thought of my actions, but I tend to believe she knows I did my best at the time, as we all grieved. I was hoping Mark would be in a better place with his grieving process. I spoke with Mark about my decision to leave, and he accepted as he promised all along but was not happy about it. My worst moment of all this was getting Kyle alone and telling him how things were going to be. It felt like I was putting him through another divorce, and I guess I was. At first, Kyle was very upset with me, as he was going to be yanked out of a family setting where we had the money for anything we wanted. I tried to explain to Kyle back then that money was not everything, and happiness is more important. As a teenager, that was hard for him to accept.

I remember his comment to this day, *"So we go back to being poor again and to struggle."* I was speechless for a moment. Mark agreed to keep Kyle grounded until I got a place for us. We had gotten him his first vehicle, a truck that Kyle enjoyed driving around and only had a few years of High School left. Mark and I agreed at this time to see each other as not to rush in making a decision. It would have to be when the children were asleep so that they could never see me there. It was to be fair to the children from this day forward and not to confuse them. It was a tough ask, as we ourselves were confused.

Mark thought at the time that he should remain single until the right woman came along. He decided to date outside the home, so the children didn't think that everyone in his life would be their new Mom. It was also going to allow Mark to build a bond with the girls.

I left and went to stay with Sonya and her family. They had a small home a few towns over from Gray Maine. The family moved a few rooms around so I could have my own room. This meant their two boys had to share a room. I was not planning to stay long, just long enough to save some money for a place to rent for Kyle and myself. Mark did let me keep my paid-off vehicle, and that helped tremendously not to have a car payment. I continued to drink heavily with my friend, being a "functioning alcoholic" as they call it. I saw Mark on and off during this time. We would meet at about 9 pm at our third story bar area and continue to drink and spend a passionate time together.

Although looking back at it now, I realize that it was not allowing him to move on, as he chose not to at that time. I stayed with Sonya and her family for about six months and then started looking for rentals. Maine is very popular for its lakes, and I always wanted to live beside a lake. I found this great cabin on the lake. We actually had a lakefront property that came with a paddle boat and two kayaks. Kyle moved into the cabin on the lake with me. As per the agreement, we only lived there on a seasonal schedule. It was from September to June. We had to move out during the summer so the family could rent it out for three times the amount.

We moved in, and Kyle could now drive to school as he had the truck. I worked 12-hour shifts in home health as Kyle would come and go as needed. He continued to do well in school and meet a very small but great group of friends. I continued to see Mark on and off and date here and there as I did not know where my life was headed, but I was happy. Well, in all honesty, I seem to be the happiest when I am single and on my own.

One stormy night, I was up visiting on the third floor of Mark's home as we usually did, and someone came up the stairs and said, *"Oh, I see why you have not answered my text messages, you are busy!"* I looked up, surprised to see another woman. She proceeded to say, *"You must be Liz, and I realize you do not know about me, do you?"* She proceeded to tell me that she knew who I was and that she had even looked me up on Facebook. I let her know that I did not know her. I had asked Mark to let me know when he started seeing someone for us not to get together anymore. It was unfair to her, the kids, and myself for him to see both of us. I definitely did not want to hurt anyone else.

The three of us talked for a while. It was determined that we could not see each other again if he wanted to move on and allow this new woman in his life to be able to get close to him and see if she is the best person for him and the children. She asked me to please stay out of their lives; she stated, *"He still loves you, and if this continues, I don't have a chance."* I let her know I would definitely go by her wishes, and also let her know that we had been through a lot together and saying goodbye forever would be hard, but will be done. I wanted the best for him and the kids. I was not the right person for him, and it wasn't just predictions, but experience; I had already given some of my years to him and the kids.

I let her know that we went through a lot of grieving together and hoped she was willing to continue to help him. She let me know at that time that she felt he drank too much and I agreed with her. I told her we both had been drinking too much, and the kids needed better than that. She told me she had a few young kids, too, and I told her she might be the perfect one for him and the kids. She was the more motherly type who still had years to raise the children together, which was something she had in common with

Mark. I was not the right person for the long haul, and we both knew it. I was more of the mistress type refusing to take the wife's role in his life. He needed to move on, and in fact, so do I! She left us to have a brief discussion. At first, I was devastated that a stranger would tell us we could not be friends or contact one another again. We both understood why and knew what we needed to do. We remained friends on Facebook, so I could see the children grow up. We said goodbye to each other and never turned back. It was time for me to focus on myself and raising Kyle through his last few years of High School.

I continued to work and often changed jobs trying to keep up with the bills. I even worked four jobs at one time to make ends meet. Kyle and I loved the cabin on the lake. We moved in and out season after season for those few years. The job I had as Director of Nursing was a few hours away in Northern Maine. I had to stay there all week. Kyle was 17 by now and stayed in the cabin by himself during the week. Kyle was very disciplined, and he had been waking up and going to school on his own for many years.

The job only lasted for almost six months due to the distance. I wanted to be there for Kyle, and the job was not allowing me to do so. During this time, I did date online, as the urge to meet people had never died on me. I did not have time to go out socially. I had run into Mark, and his new girlfriend in the grocery store as the town was very small. The kids did not see me, and they all seemed happy together. Eventually, they moved away, and the opportunity to run into them was slim to none. I believe Kyle still visited on occasion.

I started to date here and there. At the time, I chose to date guys younger than me as I still looked ten years younger than my age – thanks to the good genes. I was trying to keep my happiness on a larger scale of life. I found I had a few different ones and would see them occasionally as my jobs were taking up most of my time. During this time, I did meet one guy I started to see more frequently. It was Robert, and he lived a few towns over. He was in construction and had been building his own home when we met. On our first date, we met near my home, the cabin at the time, at a local neighborhood bar. Now I admit I have made some bad choices in life, like who hasn't!

Kyle was home asleep as it was late, so I decided to take Robert home. We had left his car at the bar and was to return him to the car in the morning, so Kyle would not see his car the following morning! I was trying to date secretly; Kyle had been through enough with the Mark situation. So we sneaked in the cabin, and it was winters, so it was very cold. Kyle slept downstairs in one of the bedrooms next to mine. The whole upstairs was blocked off at the time to savor the heat downstairs as using propane for heat was as expensive as the rent.

We needed to conserve as much as possible. The floors had a slight creek in them, and we tried to be quiet. We snuck in successfully and acted like we were teenagers in the house having sex while my son slept in the next room. He even had to put a sock in my mouth! The next morning Kyle let me sleep and got ready for school and drove off that snowy day. I eventually took Robert back to his car, and we continued on with our day. This relationship went on and off for the next five years, and so it was time for Kyle's High School Graduation.

Chapter 10
Me and Maine

As Kyle was about to graduate from High School, my ex and extended family came out to stay in the cabin. They met Robert at the time. Gladly for me, Kyle liked him for the most part. Since he had to pick a college, he let me know that he wanted to attend the University of Maine and stay with his friends here. Although I had planned to return to California after Kyle graduated High School, I decided to change my mind.

I had been in Maine for a while and had somewhat established in the town. I would not leave Kyle and move across the country even though he felt that would be okay without me. During his senior year, he and his High School friends were planning a trip to Italy. All his friend's parents had the money, while on the other hand, I was a struggling single Mom. I must give his Dad credit for taking care of some finances if we needed them, such as buying Kyle a car as his truck had broken down and was not worth fixing. He also assisted with the propane bill if needed.

I was living my lifestyle above my means of wanting Kyle to have everything he wanted. Kyle also got a job and started to take care of his expenses as much as he could. He was and still is a very financially responsible person. He sure gets that from his Dad. We had a meeting with the parents who wanted to take a chosen few to Italy for their senior trip. I was the only single Mom, but like by Kyle's friends as they loved staying at the cabin with him. I would provide a safe place for them to play video games, eat pizza, and spend the night. I finally met some of the parents who said: *"You must be Kyle's Mom, thank you for providing a fun environment for the kids, they love going and talk about the cabin often."*

Kyle's Dad and I agreed to allow Kyle to go on the trip to Italy with his friends. We always wanted him to experience life to the fullest. I believe it was Karma as when he was young, we used to take his friends to Disney Land frequently even if they couldn't afford it. Now I could not provide this trip to Italy, and fortunately, one of the friend's parents paid for all the kids to go. Kyle finally graduated from High School and was getting ready to go to college. At that time, the cabin was to be ready for the summer tenants, and I decided to move in with Robert. We had a lot of fun, and both liked riding motorcycles, going to casinos, and cooking together.

We lived downstairs of his beautiful home as he was still working on the portion upstairs. He even had a Harley parked by the bed downstairs! I was then working as a home health nurse, and the cases were two hours one way. Anyone who has lived in Maine will understand how bad snowstorms can be. There is a lot of ice, and I managed to travel daily for months in that weather. Robert also had a plowing business along with construction. I would frequently go on the plowing trips with him in the early morning hours or late at night, depending on the storms. It was something we could do together.

Kyle would come home on and off and stay with us as his house had a third floor with a bathroom; he stayed up there. He seemed to enjoy his own space – peaceful and quiet. After a year or so, I started feeling smothered, and Robert even asked me to stop spending a happy hour with my girlfriends. There were times I would drive pretty drunk and stumble into the house. Robert was trying to keep me safe. I did meet him halfway and only had a happy hour twice a month instead of weekly. During this time, Robert had a grandchild, and he was estranged from his children for some time when I had met him.

I tried to get them closer to him as he needed to see his grandchildren. He had three children – two boys and a girl. He seemed closest to his daughter, which I analyzed through a few family reunions that I had planned for him. Robert seemed like a loner, and I am not quite sure why I seemed to attract loners, maybe to rescue them and bring them out of their shell or maybe to bring me in a little from my wild side. So we managed to see the granddaughter quite a bit, and Robert once told me that I taught him how to be a great grandfather to her. We even would take her overnight at times.

Robert was one of the few people in my life who saw alcohol as an issue, enough to assist me in getting into a program. I decided to take some time off work and focus on trying to quit drinking and enter an outpatient program. So I took some time off, about two months at the time, and was accepted into the program. I did not meet the criteria for inpatient rehabilitation at the time. I entered the program with hesitation as I felt, *"I am not that bad to need rehab."* As you know, I had gone to a rehab program earlier in life. I needed to admit I had a problem and that I needed to really work on it. I went during the day from 9 am to 3 pm for about six weeks. I learned a lot about myself during that time. The thing was everyone in there with me had several DUI's, lost children and husbands, and were court-mandated. I was probably the only one who went in there voluntarily. The issue was I had not "reached my bottom," as they say. When you think about it, it is more like a matter of when not if for me, when I may get a DUI. I could not afford nor ever want to lose the nursing license that I had worked so hard for. My profession was my life, and I have always been able to keep the law out of my life.

I went through individual and group counseling for those six weeks. My individual counselor met with me three times a week and did let me know that I was a very functioning alcoholic, but I was heading toward disaster especially drinking and driving, and binge drinking on weekends, which was potentially more dangerous than drinking daily. As I said earlier, my job as a nurse has always been very important to me, so I chose to drink only on weekends for quite some time with Happy Hour once in a while during the week.

I thought that it did not affect my work week. The counseling made me realize that I did lose my family and even a few great friends because they could not watch me spiral downhill with this addiction. Kyle saw me drinking once in a while and would be concerned about my drinking and driving. One time I remember while living at the cabin on the lake, Kyle and I were both out that evening. It was snowing, and there was lots of black ice on the road. He was out with friends, and I was on a binge weekend. So I decided I wanted to go home before the bar closed down. I was about half a mile from the cabin as my SUV hit the black ice. I was pretty drunk and wound up going up a snowbank and hitting a telephone pole but was able to drive off the snowbank and finish driving to the cabin. The next morning Kyle told me he and his friend hit black ice on that same road to the cabin, and their windshield in the jeep had broken. I had pieces of the telephone pole stuck on the driver's side and had to replace that whole side panel of the car.

To tell you the truth, I thought I hit a mailbox, not a telephone pole, so obviously I was more messed up then I thought. Those six weeks of rehab, I was sober and learning more about the disease of alcoholism and my addiction. I did feel very lucky to be still alive, and I had not hurt anyone or was not in prison. It was awakening at the time, and I believe I learned that alcohol and I are enemies. I also made excuses as alcoholics, as the addictive personality does often, that I was a social drinker only on weekends, and I enjoyed social time with my friends, and it was so much part of my life. Basically, I was not totally convinced I could stop drinking forever.

I was already feeling isolated from my friends but had Robert's support. I let my family and friends know that I had quit drinking once again and was working through issues. My family and friends at the time were very proud of me. Kyle and Robert came to a session with me when we had a family day. We were in a circle and Kyle was asked if my drinking had affected his life, he responded *"not really"* only because I kept my drinking outside the home, but he knew I was out drinking with friends and would ask me to be careful. I was a little relieved by his answer; he always supported me and, in a sense, looked out for me while living his own life. I introduced him to drinking, but he drank with friends in safe places, including my home.

I became where I felt I was not myself anymore and isolated myself from all my friends. In all honesty, I did miss my old life. I also needed to get back to work. I got a job at a nursing school as a clinical instructor 40 hours a week; it was in Portland, Maine, almost an hour away from Robert's house. Now I was out again and socializing, and it was not long before I wanted to go to Happy Hour and get my life back. I thought as many alcoholics do that, I could just go back to drinking socially. It was not long before I wanted my own place again. I went looking for rentals again, and my dream was to live by the ocean. I found another rental that was seasonal on the ocean. Kyle was in college and came home frequently. He had several places he could stay or stay with me wherever I was there.

I let Kyle know that I had rented a place on the ocean; it was off-season and very cold, but the soothing sound of the waves put me to sleep most nights as my bedroom window was the view of the ocean. I even walked the ocean daily before work – it was cold but invigorating. As most of us feel, the sound of the waves is soothing and gives you peace at times. I continued with my life and Robert, and I remained friends. We saw each other a few times here and there he even stayed the night with me at the beach. He did not like the beach or water as I did. So we started seeing each other again, and I stayed less and less at the beach house but continued to pay rent. Kyle stayed there a few times before I ended that lease of seven months and moved back in with Robert. We were on and off for about five years, and Kyle stayed with us several times. He even worked with Robert in his construction business, helping him do roofing. He taught Kyle what real hard work and good work ethics. I went and lived with different friends every time we broke up for a short time. We both loved motorcycles, and we went on rides often.

One particular ride was where we followed the Vietnam Wall from Maine to New Hampshire Stateline. There were about 5000 bikes involved, and we were in the last part of the pack. We were going about 40 mph, and Robert took his eyes off the road for a second as people were on the overpass waving and yelling. We hit the bike in front of us, and I flew off the bike over three lanes of traffic, but there was no traffic as it was held for the bikes to get through, so thank god and my friend Julie. I believe she was my guardian angel at that time. My friend was driving her bike behind us, and she later on described to me what she saw as I did not remember flying through the air. By the way, my friend sold her bike after that and did not ride again. So she explained to me what she saw. I flew off the bike to the leftover three lanes of what would have been traffic as described above. She described me as going into a fetal position, and I tucked and with momentum rolled for what seemed like a long time. I could hear bikes driving by, and a few stopped to see what happened. The rule is to keep going as not to have multiple accidents. I finished rolling and remember trying to figure out what happened and where I was. I tried to sit up, and by then, I had several people around me. Of course, I was in a state of shock.

I remember not being sure if I had hurt my head or back. My first thought was paralysis, so I started to move my legs, arms, fingers, and toes. I was NOT paralyzed! Just before taking off from our last pit stop, I had taken off my gloves, as it was a warm day, so my hands seemed to be sore. I looked at them, and because I had hit the pavement so hard, it seemed like I had holes in my hands. Someone there was trying to put dry gauze on them, which I wasn't letting them. They said, *"Are you a nurse or something?"* I let them know

I was while waiting on the paramedics. I noticed my boots were shredded to my toes and did save my feet from any injury. I had lots of road rash on my back because I had a shorter leather jacket, and it came up while I was rolling on the highway. I could definitely feel the pain in my back as well as my hands. I wore jeans, and I had a hole in the knee with a small scrape on my knee. I had to have someone tell me where Robert was, and it turned out he lowered the bike and had no injuries. The rider of the bike he hit broke his leg. I remember calling out his name and looking for him. He finally ran down the road and found me with a small crowd of people around me. I was so happy he was okay. I was not sure of my injuries at this time. I asked Robert to call Kyle because he was supposed to meet us for lunch later that day. While we waited for Kyle, I was getting scans and x-rays to verify any injuries internal or external. I swear, sometimes I wonder if I have nine lives!

I did not wear a helmet, and neither was it a law in Maine at the time. It was really a stupid choice on my part. A guardian Angel looked over me, and so I had no internal injuries in my spine or head. I had the road rash on my back and on the hands. The ER tried to clean out the gravel as much as possible and gave me antibiotics. They wrapped me up in gauze, and I felt like a mummy. The motorcycle was not in the condition to be driven home. Kyle finally arrived at the ER and was very upset, especially on finding out that I was not wearing a helmet. I remember him saying to Robert, *"She is all I got, and I need her to be safe."* It did add anxiety to Robert as he felt at fault. We were all thankful for not having any significant injuries. The physician was very surprised and told Kyle, *"Your mother is so lucky, and someone must be watching out for her, and she must be here to do more work here on earth as a nurse."* I agreed as I worried about my clients in the home health-setting that I needed to see that week. Kyle drove us home, and Robert, for several weeks, and had to work on getting the remaining gravel out of my back and hands. He put the motorcycle up for a long time after the accident.

Chapter 11
Goodbye, Maine!

Goodbyes are never easy, but sooner or later, we have to let go of our old connections to make new ones.

Finally, the time had come for me and Robert to walk separate ways. The reason was the same – feeling smothered and isolated from friends again.

I moved into a condo telling myself that I was to stay there until I left Maine for California. All I was waiting for was Kyle's graduation from college. I dated on and off, but only for friendships and nothing serious. I always had it in the back of my mind that I was relocating in the near future. Resuming the "happy hour," my time was well spent with my girlfriends. My job was going well with the nursing school, and I also held down a few home health assignments for extra income. It really helped me pay my bills. I continued to live paycheck to paycheck but was very happy. It seems the most joyous times I've had were always when I am single.

It's not that male companionship isn't satisfactory, but to have full time is what exhausts me. Please do not get me wrong; I love spending time with men, but on my terms! I was lucky enough to meet a few men that were although a little younger but were on the same page as was I – "friends with benefits," as they call it. One of them was a lobsterman, and I only saw him every 4 to 6 weeks. It was when he came in from the sea. We enjoyed each other's company, and there was plenty of lobster I got for myself and my friends. They were the best lobsters in the world!

There was another gentleman who worked at Lindt chocolates, and well, all my friends love chocolate! When I got the chance to see him once or twice a month, he brought me bags of chocolate. I also met a few here and there who would take me on motorcycle rides. I was living the life!

Kyle knew I dated younger men, and he just did not want any details. I remember one particular incident when I was out with friends. It was a Friday night when I met a girlfriend that worked with me as a nurse. She worked at the hospital, where I took the nursing students for clinical. So she wanted to spend time with my friends and party with us. She was married, and her husband did not mind if she was out with me. Her husband was 30 years older than her, and she felt they no longer had much in common, but she liked his money and often bragged about it.

Normally, she was the kind of person I would have as a friend. I always have a heart for most people I meet, though. Anyhow, we had all been drinking at the local watering hole, when all of a sudden, one of my guy friends asked me if we wanted some cocaine. I had not done cocaine in years, but my girlfriend was like, *"let's do it."* Later, I found out that she used to dabble in it all the time. Anyway, we went in my car, and I was driving it. Around 1:00 am, we reached one of my friend's house to pick it up. He brought the cocaine, which we put it in the middle console of my car. Now, I was drunk driving and had possession of cocaine in my vehicle! As I pulled out of the driveway and got driving down the road, a police car began following us.

My girlfriend in the back seat began screaming, *"Oh my God, a cop is behind us."* I requested her to be quiet so that I could concentrate on my driving. Honestly, for a moment, I could see my life flash before me. I could see my nursing license being taken away and jail time! After a few but very long minutes, the police car passed us. I was so relieved! We went to my guy friend's house and played bowling on the video game. Of course, we each did a few lines at first. My girlfriend did not pitch in any money for the cocaine, despite being the richest in our lot. It was around 5 in the morning, when we realized that all the cocaine was gone. It turned out she had snorted all the rest of it. She had a history of high blood pressure and began to panic due to the overdose. She just wanted to go home. I told her I was not driving anywhere until later the next day and that she can call for a ride. As some of you might know, it is hard to fall asleep on cocaine, and you feel like crap when it's coming down. The next day at about 3 in the afternoon, I took her home. We all felt we were a little used by her to get the drugs. She was my friend, and I just accepted things the way they were.

I also had a friend of mine who had left her husband and needed a place to stay. She and I had been friends for 3-4 years by then. I had stayed at her place when I was in need, and I had the opportunity to thank her for her support. I was always willing to help a friend in need, anyway. Kyle liked the condo and stayed there often. When he came home on breaks from college, he would see his friends and me there. I would get his laundry done, as Mom's do, while he skied or went to the lake with his friends depending on the season. Kyle was just like me, a social butterfly! I continued working as a clinical nursing instructor at a local hospital for 40 hours a week. I was always meeting new people.

I was always in contact with my sisters, and we decided to visit our biological mother together. We met in upstate NY, taking the train into the city. I remember my sisters had not been to the big city, and neither had they traveled much at the time. We got into the city late in the morning and caught a cab to the hotel. We had to wait to check-in as it was too early. The hotel held our luggage until check-in, and so we decided to explore the city. There is so much in the city within just blocks of walking. We planned to spend the first day touring the city and then visiting our biological mother the next day. We were also going to meet with Barb, one of our half-sisters, later that evening.

Now it was as early as 10:30 am. My youngest sister, who did not drink much at the time, decided it would be a good idea to start drinking and loosen up. I was kind of surprised, but as you know, I would drink for any reason! We decided to go to the famous Hard Rock bar in the city. Very few people were there as it had not even been lunchtime. We chose hard liquor drinks. We were having fun talking about how nervous we were to approach our biological mother together. We promised to support each other, and none of us were sure what we were going to talk about with her. I wanted to ask about a few incidences to see if my memories were correct. My two sisters were unsure of what they wanted to get out of this trip. Our biological mother did deserve a visit from us as it was her only dream for years to see her three girls. I believe we all got something out of this particular trip.

Anyway, we continued to party and got pretty drunk. The bartender took pictures of us and had fun with us that day. There came a time after several hours of drinking that we decided to explore the city some more. We were laughing so hard along the way, who knows why, but we were having a great time. I went ahead and disappeared into the crowd. My youngest sister later told me that she quickly sobered so fast and was scared they would not find me. I managed to get several blocks away and was found in a McDonald's, making friends and eating a Big Mac! I did not even like Big Macs, and I did not remember ordering it, OMG!

We managed to get through the city blocks back to our

original bar, "the Hard Rock." The place had gotten crowded as we were then well into the evening. Our sister Barb finally found us, and we were wasted by then. She had brought her girlfriend with her, and I was like, *"Which one of you is my sister?"* Until the next day, I was unable to tell which one Barb was. I definitely needed to sober up. We all finally got back to the hotel. All five of us were pretty drunk as we all drank together for several hours that evening once Barb found us in the big city of NY!

We were a little loud in the lobby, and my younger sister was trying to herd us all with little attention to our drunkenness; it did not work. We got to the room, after which I wanted to go to the pool and get into a hot tub. I somehow found my bikini and at least had the whereabouts to put it on! We went to the pool and acted like fools in front of families that were present there. My sister Barb went in the pool with her panties and bra! We finally left the pool area and made it back to the room. On the way to the room, a few girls wanted us to party in their room. My middle sister, I believe, had alcohol poisoning and was puking in the bathroom. My little sister was trying to get me off the phone as I was inviting those girls to our room. Barb and her girlfriend were wasted too and were trying to lie down and end the crazy evening. We agreed that everyone needed to settle down and get some sleep the next day when we were going to see her. I believe my middle sister slept in the bathroom as she continued to puke through the night. We had two queen beds and a pullout bed in our room. Barb slept on the pullout bed; somehow her girlfriend slept with me on the queen bed, I don't remember her in the bed, as I passed out shortly after lying down on it. My youngest sister slept in the other queen bed, waiting on my other sister to get out of the bathroom. In the morning, I remember smelling urine and vomit! My sister never came out of the bathroom. Barb's girlfriend had urinated during the night in my bed due to being so drunk. I remember thinking I have never peed on myself with all the drinking I have done over the years.

I could not function and just stayed in bed that whole next day watching Lifetime movies with Barb and her girlfriend. My other two sisters had sobered up enough to walk around and take some bus ride to Times Square and back. We could not visit our biological mother that day because none of us could function properly. It was one of the longest and most hungover days of my life! I felt like crap, but I did not puke at all, and just got through it. The room still had lingering urine and vomit smell, so we had housekeeping skip our room because we were so embarrassed. We did later in the day ask for new linens and cleaned up the place. We all showered and finally had something to eat and planned to have a quiet night before seeing our biological mother in the morning.

The next day when we checked out of the hotel, I remember the hotel staff saying, *"Oh I remember you girls from the other night, you were loud and had entered the pool area and devastated some family."* We apologized for our behavior and went on with our day. I remember pulling up on the street where Barb and our biological mother lived. I looked up as we were getting out of the house and saw her on a balcony. She was watching us get out of the car. I believe we were all a little nervous. We all got inside the apartment and said hello and gave hugs.

Our biological mother thought it was interesting that we were too hungover to meet her the day before. She reminded us that alcoholism ran in the family on both sides. We were doomed! Our biological father died early in life in his forties of alcoholism and was drunk when he passed away. We spoke to her a little bit about our lives and the foster care system. We tried to keep it positive as we knew she suffered enough over the years and spend a lot of time looking for us. She was so happy to see us, and I did not want to ruin her happiness. She was proud of how we all turned out, successful, and had children that were doing well. There were mixed emotions for all of us.

We ate a meal together. I did get the opportunity to ask her about some memories I had, and she could not believe I remembered certain things that I have shared in the earlier part of the book. I asked other questions, and it seemed her memory was not that good on certain topics or situations. I thought some of that does not matter anymore, and life goes on. I found out that we were all named after our aunts. Also, I am the firstborn, and my biological Mom was 18 years old when she gave birth to me. My aunts used to take me on the boardwalk nearby and pretend I was their child. That seems ironic since we were in the foster care system, but found out she did not share her struggles with the family back then. We all went back to the hotel and returned home the next day on Amtrak and returned to our own lives.

I went back to Maine to the condo and continued to work and date online. There were a few regulars guys I saw. I was living a busy life. Also, I was planning a trip to the Caribbean for the holidays. It was on my bucket list to spend Christmas there. My girlfriend that worked with me at the local hospital with the students wanted to go with me. We were friends for about a year now, and I had been to her house several times for dinner. I had also been to the condo that her husband had at the beach. She spoke with her husband, and he told her to go and have a good time.

A few days before Christmas that year, which was a wintery, snowy night, I spent the night and left my car at her house as her husband took us to the airport early the next morning. We arrived in the Caribbean early afternoon and got to the resort. It was fabulous weather as we left Maine in a snow storm. We checked into the resort, and we each had our own bungalow. We went and unpacked, and I just wanted to get in my bikini and get on the beach as soon as I could. I did do that, and she did not want to go to the beach right away since she wanted to look around the resort and plan to get tickets for some day trip adventures.

She returned a few hours later with some tickets that she had bought and she said I needed to give her my share of the money. I started feeling like I brought the wrong person; it felt like a marriage! I went on vacation to just chill and not make plans for every minute! I tried to explain to her that I did not want to go on a day trip. There were several restaurants on the resort property, and she even wanted to set up dinners for the next week. I agreed to one night at a certain restaurant. So we had all our IDs, passports, and money in one locked box, which was in her room. We thought we would be doing most things together that week.

The first few days went well as we went on a few excursions together. On Tuesday night, we went out into town, where a taxi picked us up, taking us to a few local bars. A few of the bars were on the beach, and one bar actually had swings that you swing on. It was fun, and we had a great time. We went back to the resort together in the taxi, and the driver was very handsome. On the way back to the resort, she told the driver to come back and get me after he was done with his shift. At first, I was like you putting us on a date, but I agreed, and so he picked me up later that evening. He asked me what I wanted to do. I told him this was his town, so he was the one who had to show me around. We went downtown for a while and hit a few bars, did some dancing, and basically understood that we wanted to spend some time together. We wanted to have sex. He took me to this place that had a metal gate. Once that opened, and we entered, I saw it was a bunch of hotel rooms. Before you go in, we stopped at this window and got us a few beers each! As we pulled in and the gate closed, I got a little nervous at first, but I was not scared of him; his name was Jose. I just did not expect it would go down in this fashion.

We went to a room, and he said, *"I need a shower."* He took off his clothes and had a fabulous male body; he had muscles too. I felt them while we were slow dancing. He wrapped in a towel and turned on the shower. I was waiting for him, and the room door had a small opening, almost like a mail slot. I was surprised when someone came by and threw two condoms through the slot. It was nice. I was laughing to myself like who does this!

We spent a few hours together, and then I realized this was a place by the hour. We got back in the car, and it seemed like forever to wait for the gate to open. It turned out that the gatekeeper was asleep! It finally opened, and he returned me to the resort. I woke up the next day to meet my girlfriend for breakfast, and she asked me about my date with the taxi driver. We laughed about the story, and we both decided I was lucky he was not a serial killer. On Wednesday the same week, she went on a day trip, and I stayed on the beach most of the day drinking watered-down Pina Coladas. We agreed to meet at an Italian restaurant later that evening.

I was a little sunburned, but took a cool shower and met her at the restaurant for dinner. I was still a bit buzzed from drinking all day. We started by talking about our day, and then she started asking me weird questions that I did not expect as she knew me pretty well, at least to what I thought. She actually started to question my lifestyle of dating and partying all the time. I let her know that my life was totally content without a man. She continued to bash me about dating online and some of my decisions and friends I hung out with. As you know, she wanted to be a part of my single life and go with me occasionally. I could not figure out why, all of a sudden, this was an issue.

I defended myself and really did not have to. I decided to try to see where it was coming from by asking her a few questions. I was on my vacation and felt like I was on trial. I started to say things like *"Okay, let's talk about your life for a minute, are you happy?"* I let her know, I felt she was not happy, and as a friend was just making an observation. She flew off the handle, called me names, and left the table. I was like what the heck just happened. I was surprised by her reaction, to say the least. I could figure out that I had hit a nerve, and it was true that she wasn't happy with her life.

I did know they slept in separate rooms, and she drank wine each night to fall asleep. The rest of the week was interesting, to say the least. I finished dinner and tried to contact her. I knocked on the door to get my money and ID out of the locked box in her cottage. She took forever to answer and then threw my stuff out the door! She then slammed the door, and I did not see her until at the airport several days later to go home. I was on vacation alone for a few days. It worked out great as I am okay with being on my own, I always have been able to make friends anywhere I go. I love the beach and spent my days there, walking on the beach and lying in the sun.

In the evenings, I would go to the resort activities as it was the holidays, so there were many arts and craft shows conducted there. I also attended holiday festivities, which included singing and dancing. I met a few people at the Tiki bars at the resort. The day had arrived to go home, I knocked on her door to see when she was going to the airport, and she still did not answer. I went to the lobby to catch the shuttle, and the concierge desk had asked where is the person I was traveling with, that we needed to go together as a safety precaution. They needed accountability for everyone going in and out of the resort.

I let them know what I thought that she might be already at the airport. She was not answering her phone when I tried to find out. I proceeded to the airport. I was going to the terminal, and I saw her sitting there. I asked her about taking me to her home from the airport as my car was at her house, and she responded rudely, *"You can find your own ride to my house."* I called Kyle to ask him to pick me up from the airport. We got on the plane and were sitting across from each other in the aisle seats. I tried to speak to her, but she just kept ignoring me. We landed in Portland, Maine, in a snow storm. Her husband thought it was ridiculous that Kyle would come to get me in the storm, and they were going home where my car was. She caved in and said, *"Fine, let's take her, then."*

There was silence on the way home, and it was very awkward for the three of us involved. I got in my car and thanked them for the ride and drove home. I had a great time regardless of her attitude. I still had to work with her and the students. I was hoping she would be cordial for the student experience. The next week I went back to work, and she was there too. As usual, I approached her to ask about having the medication cart for the students to pass the medications. She refused to count the meds and threw the keys at me. The students were surprised at her behavior as we were friends before the trip. I pulled her aside and asked if she could please put her feelings aside during the time I am there with the students. She finally did, and our time together with the students ran smoother.

It was funny because some of the other staff members I knew said, *"Oh, it is your turn for her to treat you like she treated a few others before you."* I was like, why didn't someone warn me! I guess I had to learn who she indeed was the hard way. I still killed her with kindness until I left the state of Maine to go back to California, as were my plans 6-8 months later.

It was getting closer for Kyle to graduate from college, and my 50th birthday was approaching in April. I had a few friends who had planned to take me out for an evening of dancing in downtown Portland. It was a work night, and I wanted to end it early. We got to have too much fun, and I met a younger guy there. He wanted to celebrate my birthday with the girls and me.

The girls wanted to spend the night and go to work together in the morning. Jason and I went to the house in his truck. He was very drunk, as I was, and we drove, not proud of that at all. It just adds to the list of poor decisions I've made when drinking. The girls were in my bedroom, and Jason and I were in my spare bedroom. We got up in the morning and went to work feeling very crappy, as you can imagine. I said goodbye to Jason and made a date for later in the week. It was one of the longest days of my life, needless to say!

In the meantime, Kyle was about to graduate from college. He pinned for the second Lieutenant of the United States Army. I had to decide when to return and leave for California. I had dated Jason for about six times. There were times he would call me from the bar to pick him up and get him home safely. I did that a few times in the middle of the night until the sad news reached me. I was at work one day and got the news that he had died, wrapped his car around a tree. It was a case of drunk driving. My first thought was, why didn't he call me, and I felt so guilty for a while. There was an opportunity online to write in the book that was at the funeral home for the ones who couldn't attend. I wrote in the book and even today receive emails that come in for me to write in that book so as not to forget him. I have since forgiven myself and realized that he did not feel he needed to call me or anyone else that night. It was just one more of the many reasons to leave Maine.

Chapter 12
California Drama

My friend Lorna had not seen Kyle for some time and wanted to come to Maine to see him at his graduation. I was excited to see her. If you remember, she was the one who was with me during the early years of Kyle when he had kidney issues. She is a very special person to me; she is kind of like a Mom. I was still spending time out with friends, mostly doing binge drinking on weekends. Lorna was due to fly into Boston and then drive a few hours to Maine.

I had assured her that I would be home at the condo to welcome her. I had spoken to Lorna over the phone on the morning of her arrival. The next day, we had plans to go to college to attend Kyle's graduation. I was going out to dinner with friends and intended to be back for Lorna. My evening got busy, which meant lots of drinking, so I did not pay attention to the time. I looked down at my phone and saw that I had missed a call from Lorna ten minutes ago. I was like, "OMG, I need to call her right now."

I went outside the bar due as it was really loud inside and called her several times. I even left several voicemails apologizing and telling her to come back. I had to get to the condo right away. It was too late, and yet again, my drinking and selfishness hurt someone else. She finally left me a voicemail saying she had a friend in Boston that she would stay with, and her last words that day were only to contact her if I remained sober for a year. I had really messed up!

I went back to the bar and continued drinking. A guy I had been seeing went home with me that night. We got up the next day closer to the afternoon hours, and I needed to be at the college in a few hours. I had little time to get ready. My friend went home, and I got ready to go. I was still feeling bad for not being responsible enough to be there when my friend Lorna had arrived. I got ready and got over to the college.

I am always so proud of my son, and that day I was overwhelmed with his success. When he puts his mind to something, he succeeds over the top. I will always be proud of him, and often tell him that. He is my world and always will be. His Dad has remarried, and his new wife was also there, as was expected. When it was time to put the second lieutenant bars on his uniform, I asked his Dad's wife to join us to do the honors. It made her become a big part of Kyle's life, and so she was honored to do it. I am one who wants everyone happy. I told his wife that day that Kyle's Dad is a wonderful man and father; he's just not the one for me! It was a fabulous day as family and friends celebrated Kyle's accomplishments of graduating with a bachelor's degree and becoming an Officer of The United States Army.

Kyle was to head to Fort Benning for further training, while I had the opportunity to go back to California. I was working as a clinical instructor for a nursing program, and the company needed me to go to Northern California to be a Director Of Nursing for the school in that area. Our time had ended in Maine for myself and Kyle as we both moved to another chapter in life.

I did a trip cross country to head back to California. Everything I owned at the time, fit into my Kia Soul. I drove by myself as I often did due to not having anyone that could go. I had about five days to get across the country and traveled about 12 hours a day. I arrived in a small town in Northern California at around 9 pm. I prepaid the apartment complex in advance, so the manager was waiting on me to hand over the key. She gave me the key and walked me to my apartment. It was getting late by now, and I had to get myself some things such as a bed and shower curtain.

I went to the nearby Walmart that was open 24 hours. I was super tired but needed to go, as I also needed to buy some food. I went shopping and got household items such as brooms, toiletries, and a blow-up mattress with sheets, pillows, and blankets, to name a few. It was about 2 am before I returned to the empty apartment. I put the few groceries away, made the bed, put up the shower curtain, and took a shower. I only had a few hours of sleep before meeting my Maine Leadership at the local Nursing School to start my new job.

The next morning I drove to the Nursing School and was surprised to see that it consisted of classrooms spread out in a business center. I did not even see the name of the school anywhere. The front desk and admission personnel greeted me. They said, *"You must be Liz, we have been expecting you."* I then met with the leadership to explain the logistics of the building and classroom student numbers. I learned that there were currently five classes in session that were not catered and that the next class was to graduate in about six months. They were short of teachers, but we had classes daytime and evenings. I had asked leadership before I made the trip how messed up the school was and how much fixing it required. They had stretched the truth and told me that it was a little messed up. It turned out to be quite messed up.

That first day was a long day, as I got to meet all the five classes! I heard nothing but complaints – *how bad the teachers are, not learning anything, poor lab equipment* – and even how teachers showed up late or at times, not at all. I was thinking, *how am I going to fix all these problems, run the school, and have happy students!* I knew I had a huge challenge on my hands, and the leadership expected me to be a great leader and get things in order as soon as possible. I met all the students on the first day of both the day and evening classes. They knew I was coming for about two months and expected me to listen and do something about it. I let them know that I was one person and needed to look at the whole picture, and each class separately. It sure was going to take some time.

I spent the first few weeks looking at schedules, meeting the staff, to understand what was needed to make it a more successful program. I found out the program was in shambles and needed a new lab and equipment. I also needed to hire and fire employees in the first few months. The area the school was in was not the safest place. We had classes from 7 to 10:30 pm, and we all walked each other out each night. I had to work as a Director and teach classes at the same time. We were also looking for a new building to have the school more visible and productive. I worked with the State Board Of Nursing and attended monthly meetings as needed on the school's status as we were taking over a former school. I was happy we were moving to a new location in a better part of town and hoping that the school would be brand new. I got to be part of the plans for the new school location.

In the meantime, I had made a few local friends I met for Happy Hour each week until I had to increase my hours at the school and hardly had any time left for a social life. I dated online and was there for about six months. I met a guy my age, his name was JC, and he later became a significant part of my life. It was going to be a four-day weekend, and lately, I had not had much time off, so I was looking forward to it. It was the 4th of July, a weekend. I had plans with my girlfriends to attend the fireworks in the local area. I told my

JC I had a four day weekend, and so I had time to meet him for coffee the morning on the 4th of July. He had just bought a home and wanted me to come by, and he was going to make me coffee there. He let me know he drank instant coffee and liked Hazelnut creamer. I liked the Hazelnut creamer too. I told him I would bring my Keurig coffeemaker as I did not like instant coffee. We agreed to meet around 9 am the next morning.

I woke up and realized I only had two cups for my coffeemaker, so to calm my nerves, I had a half bottle of wine for my morning coffee! I pulled up in front of his house at about 9:15 am. I did call him to say I was going to be late. He admitted he was nervous and pacing the house, waiting for me. I went up to the front door, which he had opened as he saw me pull up, I had the coffee maker in my hand and 2 K-cups. He showed me to the kitchen, and I set up the coffee maker. He took out the Hazelnut creamer, and we had a cup of coffee while talking in the kitchen.

JC was about 5 foot 9, was bald, and had hazel eyes. He was in good shape too. He had no furniture yet except for his bedroom, neither did he have a kitchen, a dining room table, or a living room furniture. He had moved in a few months ago and had painted and replaced the carpets. It was a two-story home consisting of four-bedrooms and three-bathrooms. The house flooring was of hardwood, thus elegant. He seemed to be a neat and clean guy – something you don't find in bachelors. He was working as a cell phone tower builder. The secret to his good shape was that he climbed up several hundred feet a day and hung off the side of buildings at times.

I found his career to be interesting; I had never dated anyone in that field before. I told him a little bit about myself and the job I had at the school. He was impressed and had never dated a nurse before. He told me he did not drink at the time, and I let him know that I was a drinker and loved my girlfriend time, wine tasting, and Happy Hour. I also let him know my hours at the school were keeping me very busy and so did not have much time for dating. He told me he had a past I needed to know about, he did have some tattoos I thought might have been from prison. I did tend to go after the bad boys. He told me he was in prison about three times for getting caught making and selling crystal meth. He had been sober 15 years then. I am a person that believes in second chances, and as you are reading my story here, you see, I have been no saint. Although I have no record and have never done time, I just did not get caught. He had nine felonies, all having to do with drugs. I learned more about that part of his life as I got to know him and spend time with him. Of course, I did not know that world or ever been part of it, so I did not fully understand that lifestyle. He continued to tell me he was on the streets for eight years of his past running from the law. He said he was way past that life. It sure seemed that way from the life he lived and the way he owned his first home.

After a while, he asked if I wanted to get breakfast. I told him I did not eat breakfast. We hugged and started kissing; we found we had some chemistry, and the date lasted for four days. I had to call my girlfriends and let them know I was making my own fireworks and will see them later in the week. We watched movies, ate Chinese food in bed, and talked for hours over the next several days. It was certainly the longest first date we both ever had. I left the following Tuesday morning to go to my apartment to get ready for work. We agreed at the time that we would see each other a few days a week. I could spend a few nights at his house, and other nights at my apartment. I still had six months on the lease. I went back to work well-rested and ready to tackle the everyday grind of running a nursing school, waiting for the final move to our new school. I continued to work closely with the next graduating class as they still needed to prepare for the state boards. As I was doing that more classes were about to start. I kept telling the leadership that I needed to get a handle on the classes already in session before new classes could start. They were all about quantity versus quality.

My job was to make sure the state board results were kept up to keep the school open. I also was trying to build rapport with the staff and hire new staff. It seemed I worked more and more hours to keep the school open. I went over to JC's house after work at 10:30 pm a few nights a week and snuck into bed to snuggle as he was already asleep at that time. We decided to start dating officially. He was quite understanding, realizing I worked long hours. He came to the school in the evenings and brought me something for dinner a few days a week. The students would tease me about having a boyfriend but were happy for me. I did spend more time at the school with the students than I did at home. It was almost time to move into the new school, and the company hired a moving company to move equipment and furniture. The leadership wanted some of us employees to assist with the move and let them know where to put the furniture and equipment. I spent an entire weekend hauling books, furniture, and equipment up and downstairs. The move was also close to a new start date for the upcoming next class. It was actually on a Saturday, and the new students joined on Monday. I believe a class of 40 students was going to join us, which was the biggest class as of yet in that school. I communicated with the leadership that it was moving too fast, and we really were not ready, but they did not listen.

The new class started while some classes were finishing up. I was working 70 to 80 hours per week to keep up with teaching and directing. The students were not getting what they paid for, and me being one person could only do so much. Also, during this time, I had gone back to Maine for a week to rewrite the curriculum to match the Maine program. I worked long hours there with my Maine counterparts to get this done. The curriculum was to be approved by the State of California. I had a great administrator, but her hands were tied to what she could do for my nursing program. She was also the director of some of the other programs, including medical assistant, heating and cooling, and welding, which was a new class starting. Her department was also not fully staffed. The medical assistant instructor was hospitalized due to the stress of working too many hours.

I also was very sick for a week, and the place went to hell in a handbasket while I was gone. I came back to student complaints, and students did not go to clinical rotations. It was a mess as I had to reconnect with clinical liaisons and get the students back in the clinical setting. It was as if my absence for 14 hours a day made everybody just slack on the job, including both the students and instructors. I needed a vacation and went to Cabo with JC, after hardly seeing him for several weeks. We actually broke up and then got back together due to my work schedule and my stress level, but I was determined to do this for the students. I had to be there for them.

JC and I went to Cabo and had a great time. We had some strain between us. It was maybe because I was worried about the school and students the whole time. JC had rented a boat just for us to go fishing, and we both did catch a Marlin. I was not into fishing at that time, but I quickly learned it. It was fun. We had a great resort and enjoyed the beach, all-inclusive food, and beverages. While I was gone on vacation, results were coming in from students who had passed and not passed the State Boards. The results were of the graduating class.

After our seven-day trip, I got back home and was well rested for the time being as I knew I had to return to long hours. I got back to the news that only five out of the eleven students had passed. I was devastated as my job was to make sure that most students passed the State Boards. I know I was not there except for their last six months, but I tried to make a difference. I guess with all the other classes and responsibilities, I failed. I was talked to by the leadership, and I let them know they needed to visit my campus more often than every few months and see what was really going on. I tried to speak to them weekly about my need for help and to stop admitting new students.

The State Board of Nursing finally put a hold on new starts for the school. I was relieved and thought I could catch up. It was too late for that as other classes graduated and continued to have a low pass rate. I later found out that the leadership was back in Maine trying to save that nursing program that eventually closed and did not have the time to make sure this program in California did not close. Eventually, I got an offer to be a regional director and assist in opening more nursing programs in Northern and Southern California.

Now, this seemed crazy because we could not run the one nursing program, and they wanted eight more programs to open. I gave up the director position as another instructor took over. I was still teaching and doing clinical while waiting for these schools to be established. I did present the State Board of Nursing with the first two new programs. I went to a meeting with my leadership, who, for the first time, got to see how the state perceived our school. We were told that we could not at that time open any schools, we needed to get the one program running better and produce better state board results.

My leadership was upset with me, and I let them know if I had better leadership, this would not have happened. I put my heart and soul into this program for the students. The students demanded to meet with leadership, they reluctantly did, and I warned them it was going to be ugly. I was able as I desired to sit in one of the conversations.

The students were so upset that I was working so many hours and pulled in different directions. They asked about more and better instructors. I had hired some that only lasted a few weeks or months at a time. The program also would not pay enough for the work involved. The leadership just let them know that they were working on it. The students said that it was always there answer. The students also suggested stopping adding more classes, as the ones in the session were poorly handled. Some of the students threatened to go to the Board of Nursing if needed. I continued to do clinical and teaching seven days a week while providing the new director with my assistance. I saw this had no good ending, and we were working in circles and getting nowhere.

One day I took the students to a clinical setting. We were in our morning meeting before hitting the floor. The students were complaining that clinical was boring and that they were not learning anything. I just was at the end of my rope, and I said, *"It has been two years, and I have given all I can. I will not put up with this constant complaining anymore. We are going back to school, and you do what you want."* I went to the school, collected all my things, and left. I notified the leadership that I had enough wishing them luck for the future. I said, *"I promise you that you will be closed down shortly if you don't get it together. I gave you all I could and then some."*

I notified the new Director and let her know. She said, *"There is no way we will make it now. You held this place together."* I let her know I was sorry but needed to keep myself healthy and sane. I had lost so much weight due to not eating and stressing. It just wasn't worth it. They set me up for failure and let the students and me down. I have never walked away from a job before. I warned them over and over, and believe me, I gave it everything. I had a weight lifted as I drove away that day. I went home to JC and started another chapter of our lives.

A few days later, I received a call from leadership, asking me when I was coming back. I was like, are you kidding? They truly thought I just had to take a few days off, and I would be back. They realized as one person, I did so much, and others would not step up to the task. They finally realized my worth. I told them I was looking for a job that will value me and pay what I am worth. They asked while I am waiting on another job I could assist the director a little bit and get her up to speed. I could not believe it, but I agreed. It turned out they were not upset with me, they finally realized they were very negligent in their leadership, and that's when they let me know the Maine program had closed and lawsuits were most likely coming. The students there felt the same as the students here, paid too much for tuition and poor teaching and clinical. They also had poor state board results and finally was shut down. The State of California knew this and was now looking closely at this program and even did an audit. They finally concluded that we could finish out the classes already started but could no longer accept new students until further notice.

I assisted the director, who left as she was unwilling to put in the work and hours that I did. As you would expect, the nursing program was eventually shut down, and no further nursing programs opened. There were lawsuits, and I felt bad but had warned them all along.

I did get another job shortly after, to work about an hour away for a Nurse Case Manager position at an insurance company. It was Monday to Friday – 9 to 5. I was making more money and less stress. It was amazing as I started this new job with better pay and great leadership. They realized the stress and work I was dealing with in the past two years. When I look back, I still wonder how I did it. Anyway, I was starting to live life like a normal person. I had my weekends off, met up with friends again, and enjoyed happy hour and wineries in Napa Valley, CA. JC and I had moved in together and settled into a more normal routine. I was traveling more, though, and during the week, I barely spent an hour in the evening with JC before going to bed.

After several months, JC suggested that maybe I should stay up at my work area with a friend during the week and come home on Friday nights. I had made a few great friends at my new job, and the offer was there for me to stay at my will. JC was still working at building cell phone towers but changed companies often. It was the same work, but different companies and once in a while worked out of town. I did not see this as a problem as I enjoyed time apart as well as together. I tend to feel smothered, as you know, if someone is always in my space.

After a while, I started making more friends and continued going to the happy hour during the week. As I went home each week, JC was starting to think I was settling with my new friends and maybe even seeing other guys. I let him know I was not seeing other guys and making friends wherever I go. I told him that I was coming home to him and not anyone else. He continued to accuse me of cheating. He would call me constantly while at work and leave a million voicemails, insisting that I call him or he'd come to my workplace. I finally called him back and told him to take my word that I would be home on the weekend to pack my things. I was tired of his accusations.

I had a few friends. I took turns staying with one girlfriend who was married with two kids and another girlfriend who was divorced with two kids. The divorced one and I were not good together as we would drink and party too much together. I have always been a drinker but had a rule that it would not interfere with my nursing profession. I needed to stay with my girlfriend with a stable marriage and the two kids to focus on other things besides getting into the drama of a divorced couple. I did get in their drama for a bit and tried to be there for my friend, she finally met someone, and he took over. I went to stay with my other girlfriend and even would babysit for the kids while they went on date night.

I continued to go back and forth and visit friends and even spoke to JC now and then. One weekend I visited a girlfriend named Phyllis, and I was supposed to see JC while I was there just to say hi. I went to a winery, and we met some other nurses in the area. We stayed until closing and unfortunately had too much to drink. I made a bad choice and thought I could drive. We had gotten there a little later than usual and parked in a different area than usual.

On the way out, I got in the driver's seat and Phyllis in the passenger seat. I drove forward and started to rain, but I was stuck in what seemed like a maze. The car stuck in the mud. Fortunately, I had a shovel in the back of my car. I believe it was there from the time I lived in Maine. It sure did come in handy that night. I remember JC calling and saying, *"Where you at?"* I replied, *"Not sure. It seems like we are in a maze!"* It seemed like forever until we got out onto a road.

We drove the 45 minutes to the next drink, anyone who does party knows it could be a long day and night of drinking. I am not proud of that night and once again got away with not hurting myself or others. We got to another bar that we knew well, and we walked in, and they served us a Margarita with extra Tequila. They should not have served us as we walked in all muddy and still buzzed. We finished our drink, and each drove home in our own vehicle as we left Phyllis's vehicle in the parking lot and rode together to the winery. I pulled into the driveway at JC's and went into the house. JC was questioning me even though I was not currently living there, but he was still and always concerned about my drinking and driving. I apologized as usual, and we went to bed. The next morning, we had to get new tires on my vehicle.

I walked out of the house and saw the car in the daylight. The tires and tire wells were caked with mud, and the passenger side of the vehicle was all banged up. I was trying to figure out what had happened. I had to clean the car even to get the tires. I called Phyllis to discuss my findings, then we both realized we had driven through the vineyards at the winery! I was devastated not to remember driving through them; then, the 45-minute drive home was in a blackout!

I had to replace the side panel of my vehicle on the passenger side. I went to my winery every three months to pick up my wine bottles and do a wine tasting with my friends. On our next visit that Phyllis and I went to in those three months, we approached the bar to start tasting, and they talked about someone getting away with driving through the vineyards. We picked up the wine and did a very little wine tasting. I finally just canceled my membership and took the temptation away.

Chapter 13
Choosing Torture

JC and I were talking again about getting back together. He asked me to come and see him one weekend – he had a surprise for me. I always wanted to go to Monterey for the day and visit the aquarium. I spent the weekend with him and went to Monterey and, of course, the aquarium. We were like teenagers and had a great weekend. I headed out Monday to work, leaving behind plans to talk some more that week. I was talking with my girlfriend I was staying with, and she agreed that trying again may be worth it.

I packed all my stuff and moved back in with JC, and we even discussed that I might need to move back closer to home and leave the job. I wanted to save the relationship. I told him we could discuss it, but I would really like to have another job lined up. I went back and forth to the job daily and home every night. One day JC spoke with me about sharing his past with me. It had to do with the drug "meth" or "Ice," as known on the streets. I remember looking at him and thinking about what will that do for us.

We were just getting back together again and had our own issues before introducing drugs to our world. I also reminded him that I had never been in that world, or as I learned "the game." He spoke of his past, forcing me to figure out the motive behind the discussion. He felt the only thing we had not shared were things that were important in his life. I was speechless for several minutes, and then I agreed to try it for only a short time and on the weekend only.

I had no idea what I was getting into! So, JC had a friend that used to manufacture the drug with him 20 years ago. We took him fishing all the time, and it turned out he was actively using it in the last 30 years. JC also spoke of the drug and what it was like on and off over the few years. I did not think much of it because JC and I did not even think it was of any relevance to our lives. I listened to their stories and kept moving.

I guess something triggered in JC to ask me to try it. He knew I had a very addictive personality, but my drug of choice was alcohol. JC spoke with his friend about getting us the drug. At first, his friend was truly surprised as JC wanted to use it after 15 years of sobriety. What was even more surprising for him was to have JC introducing it to me.

We all knew I had never tried meth ever in my life! We went on the boat that his friend had at the marina. I remember walking on the boat and seeing a few guys there. JC took a hit with the pipe and was showing me how to do it. I was a non-smoker all my life and so had asked him to shot-gun it into my mouth. I knew I would eventually learn how to do it. It immediately made me feel weird but relaxed. We did a little more with the boys and took our own to the house.

This was a Friday night, and I had to be to work on Monday. JC had purchased what seemed like a blow torch and several glass pipes. The pipe was round at the end with a small hole in the top. You have to torch and melt the crystals, and the smoke comes out of the hole in the top. You roll the pipe while you suck in the drug, but make sure not to spill the hot melted drug out of the hole as you roll it. It makes me a little sick to my stomach as I relive this part of my life.

We went home and smoked for the whole night. I also learned to smoke cigarettes at the time as it went together with meth to enhance the high. The time went by so fast, and I was too high to realize it. This drug heightens your sex drive to a level that I never knew existed. We already had a good sex life, but I believe JC thought we should experience it together. Being in love with that person was to make it all the more special. It turns off your sleep center as it may be made with high amounts of caffeine. The more you do it, the longer you stay up. I also could not eat on this drug, so I lost weight quickly, even if I just did it on the weekend or a five-day binge. That first-weekend binge, I did not know I would not get to work until Wednesday. I had to call in because I could not sleep; we would try to gage when we should have stopped smoking it. We still went to work.

It was so addictive and new to my brain. The first week I returned to work on Wednesday, my friends knew something was up. This drug, as is the case with many others, makes you lie and cover it up. I told them I was tired and not feeling well. My weight loss was mentioned, and I denied it. I went to work and put in my two weeks notice and was currently looking for a job closer to home. My colleagues, including my boss at the time, thought that if I wanted to save my relationship, I needed to go closer to home. I only worked two days that week, and it was Friday already. We both got home and wanted to smoke again! The first two weeks were crazy, but we both were starting to miss work. I finished at my job, had time between jobs, and was eagerly waiting for the three-day weekend. We had weekend plans to go fishing and just blew it off as we stayed up for 2-3 days in a row. I went to a new job interview after getting sleep and having the ability to eat something. I got the job, and it started within 4-5 days. We saw that as a perfect window of time to get high for a few days. JC started not going to work and calling in making excuses for our poor choices. We tried to live our normal lives around smoking. It was getting very difficult as we wanted the drug more and more.

When I started the new job as an Assistant Director at a nursing school, we skipped a few weekends and went back to a normal life. We both went to work five days a week and tried to stay busy not to touch the drug. It was upstairs in our closet, and we knew it, and all it took was one look at it – we were so weak. The nursing school I was working at was starting to take on the same feeling of my previous nursing school. The students all complained to me they were not feeling like they were learning anything. I spoke to the Administration, and they claimed the students were always lying and complaining.

I did not feel that job and started calling on Fridays after I hit the pipe before going to work. JC was already at work and tried to get home early, knowing I was high all day. I even made videos for JC – dancing and sexual videos. One time I burned my hands and fingers as I tried to melt the stuff. We did several more weekends in a row. I finally went to work on little sleep and had to teach the students. The drug makes your mouth very dry; I was trying to talk in class and couldn't.

At that moment, I knew I needed not to take those kinds of chances anymore. I made it through that long day, and we took a break again. I kept reminding JC that we needed to stop. We have done it long enough already. Meth does not take long to affect a person's daily life. We still had more of the drug available and continued to be weak. It was time for my 90-day review, and so I went in that day as JC had stayed home. He started to hit the pipe, waiting for me. He would text and say, *"Hurry up and get home!"*

At the end of the day, the administrator came in with a cardboard box and said, *"Your position is no longer needed, pack your things, and we will walk you out."* I have been a nurse for 28 years and never been let go. As I looked back, I realized that I had never called in either over the years as much as I had in those 90 days. I called JC and was crying as I drove in the pouring rain in that early November. He calmed me down. I remembered I would collect unemployment as they let me go, so I was technically not fired. It was a terrible time to lose my job as holidays were coming up, and we had an excuse to continue using if we wanted to. I was so upset when I got home but soon made excuses for staying home and getting high. JC felt like staying home, too, and I talked him into staying employed. We both did not need to be unemployed as we had bills, houses, and a boat to pay for!

I still had a few full paychecks coming and some money saved. I put in for unemployment right away, and they agreed to pay me. I also started looking for work right away. JC and I continued to dabble in the drug, and we finally ran out of the first batch we had gotten. I spoke with JC about meeting his friend, and I would get us some. I could not believe what I would do to get another hit. I was in the game as I learned from others I met during this crazy time of my life. I had a rule that I would go to the drug house and wait on it, no smoking it and partying with anyone but JC.

I was too scared to do it with anyone, but JC, I trusted him at that very vulnerable time and only him. I went to some very shady places with shady people who were very paranoid as we waited for the drug and dealer to arrive. There were times I was there for hours, and it really made me nervous. Once in a while, someone would ask me why I was now trying such a dangerous drug, and they kept reminding me that it will ruin my life. I let them know it was only temporary, and I will be getting off of it soon. We started to go fishing again and trying to get off of the drug. It seemed one of us would be okay to stop, and then we both caved. We were not strong enough together to stop. We were not talking to too many friends at the time. We had no company coming to the house, not that we had many visitors anyway.

One day we went fishing and actually got braver than usual and smoked on the boat just before heading home. JC had discussed we would only do it in the comfort of our home, our safe place, and never drive after smoking. We were starting to take chances outside the home, and it made me nervous. JC said he was okay to drive, and he got us home. We usually cleaned the boat and the fish on our return, but this day we wanted to get high and left the fish in the boat. This is very sad and hard to say, but we went on a three-week binge. It was a world of craziness beyond belief.

This is my perspective after spending many days and nights of hallucinations, both visual and auditory. JC had a saying; he called it "fuck it time." He just never called in and never went to work. We dove into this drug full force for weeks on end. The work truck JC had just disappeared from the front of the house. We later realized that the company came and got the truck and did not tell us. We probably would not have heard the door or answered it anyway.

I started to have hallucinations. The longer anyone stays awake, hallucinations will occur, but the drug made it worse, as you can imagine. We did not know what was in the drug we were smoking. At first, the hallucinations were centered around my life experiences. I was a nurse for a long time, so one night, the house became a nursing home setting. We had several bedrooms, and a long hallway and old-people were coming out of the rooms in walkers and wheelchairs wearing my pajamas. Crazy right? Also, I have been in the military, and one night the planes were landing in the house, and the military staff emptied cargo. There were lockers lined in the hallways of my home, and I could see and hear military personnel talking and working. I heard even the distinct noise of lockers opening and closing. The military was also out front doing military maneuvers in the street and guarding our homes. I could hear them talking through the door. As I am writing this, I realize how a lack of sleep and drug use can really affect the brain. I had no control over what hallucination was coming next. I had to keep sharing with JC what I saw in order to keep from going insane.

During this time we would also eventually get some sleep, I mean like 14 hours at a time and even eat something now and then. The only thing we could eat when we were too high was water and some crackers, which would be hard to chew and swallow as our mouth would get super dry. I remember answering the phone, and I could not even speak at times without difficulty. We had a dog at the time, and I would have to remember to let her out and even feed her. You have no sense of time on that particular drug. The drug was really based around sex. I had just gotten back with JC, and my hallucinations became sex-based with the drug being passed around – I saw and even smelled the drug. The house, especially once darkness hit, became a sex party for lack of a better word. I heard and saw people or entities as I started to call them, having sex all over the house, and our bed became so full of people I would be struggling, so I thought, to get to JC. I would feel rejected and cried many nights and begged JC to help me sleep as that was the only way these hallucinations went away. The lack of control of what is happening around me was devastating.

I knew it was not real, but it seems so real when you are in this situation. It was so bad, but I was in my craziness ordering sex toys, and they would arrive on the porch, and we would not know it for days. We even went as far as may be trying to bring a third person into the craziness, and I told JC no way as I can't even get your attention anymore at times. We even would get in arguments over something that was not happening. I was able to get a few sane and sober moments to continue to look for work, believe it or not! I remember it was Christmas Eve about 11:30, and we ran out of the stuff.

We were so desperate that we got in the car, at which point JC promised we would never leave the house all screwed up and went about an hour away to get some more. It was awful as now I was outside, and the hallucinations seemed worse. Inside the car, I saw all kinds of things and people and I thought there was no room for me. I sat in the back as JC drove. I kept seeing people on the road and kept screaming at JC not to keep hitting people. I did not want to go to jail. I was literally terrified. We got to the drug house, and a few of the shady people we knew were there. It was a three-hour wait, which seemed forever at the time.

I was so nervous and paranoid, and JC kept reassuring me that it was going to be okay. As we left the drug house that night, I will never forget seeing one of our friends huffing a paint can, and I thought he was so high he might just die right there. I can't believe that I would ever in a million years be that person. I saw JC at least in my hallucinations talking to people not there, and we both accused each other of things that were not happening. It was sad to see someone I loved to go through this, but we were going through it together.

JC and I had a bond as crazy as it was that I would never have it with anyone again! I also loved the beach and had hallucinations of a 3D beach coming up from our bedroom floor. I could clearly hear the seagulls, the water and the waves, the people lying on the beach, some playing volleyball, and if the hallucination was happy, I was okay. I think back the brain does amazing things with lack of sleep and, of course, the drugs constantly in the system.

One night it seemed like we were not in our own bedroom, and JC started to admit he was seeing and hearing things too. I was very concerned that I was the only one with vivid auditory and visual hallucinations. I did realize our brains handle things differently in each individual person. I tried so hard to stop and get some sleep, but we were so entrenched in this drug that sleep never came by easily. We even took several drugs that cause sleep, but it never worked. We had to stop! No sleep until you do! I did not know the body could stay awake that long; my heart would often be racing out of my chest. I thought I was going to die.

We would take little breaks at times. The worst thing that happened was I had made videos, as I mentioned earlier, and JC was always going through my phone and trying to use the drug as a truth serum and trying to get me to admit all the guys I saw the times we were separated. He made a mistake and sent a few of my dance videos to youtube. I received an email letting me know that they were ready for view. We were both devastated and tried to get them deleted; we were able to do it, but not before some already saw them and made comments! They also named it, "Way to go, Liz." Some of the comments were "I want whatever she is on," "Nice body," and "Wow." I am not proud of this, but it was just part of our craziness at the time.

We finally stopped for a few weeks and got some much-needed sleep. I was also interviewing for a few jobs. I landed a job at a nearby hospital as a Nurse Case Manager with a government contract and had a start date a few weeks later. In our poor decision state, we decided to have another week of craziness and get more to smoke and celebrate my new job. I told JC this would be our last time, as I did not want to lose another job! He agreed at the time. This trip, as I call it, escalated to dark hallucinations.

At night dark figures appeared, and I was very scared as JC would hold me away from the entities and let me know it was not real. I would wake up all bruised up for real and was very concerned as JC was. We decided we both got really rough with each other, and we were not remembering. That is a very scary thought, like a blackout! There were times we did not recognize each other in this deep drug-induced stupidity.

We finally stopped as I was getting ready to go back to work. I worked for about two weeks, and we were craving again. It seemed as I sobered up from it, I kept forgetting the bad part about it. I just remembered how it made me feel and JC, and I enjoyed that intimacy to a point it did not take long to remember why we needed to stop. We started again thinking, or rather the lack of thinking that we could do Friday night and quit by Saturday Morning. I found I could not go to work until Wednesday, even if we quit Saturday morning as the drug lingered in my brain and was not going to allow me any sleep!

I had this thought that quitting for a few weeks would make the drug act differently. To my surprise, it acted the same way every time! I still did not learn at the time. So early in my employment, I started to miss work lying as to why. The drug indeed makes you very deceitful and selfish. I got away with it for a while as my current employer at the time would never have thought I was dabbling in any such drug. I did go to work a few times with not enough sleep, and the hallucinations followed me to the workplace; it was very scary.

I just made it through my long day and tried to ignore them. We continued for a few more months on and off smoking. I was trying so hard to quit for good and talking to JC about it. We both were so weak at the time. I was also still smoking cigarettes daily. So this lasted about a year and a half of my life, and I was not myself. We went through several thousand dollars and much isolation from others. All my friends do not know me to be that way. I am usually very outgoing and social. At this time, we were still planning to get married. In our drug-induced minds, we thought we were perfect for each other.

I am now going into the last time we touched the drug, and this last time was an incident where I was tricked. We had been sober for two months and was on a journey to get married and never touch it again. We were fishing as we often did, and JC continued to take his childhood friend that he used to make meth with on our fishing trips on weekends. I had asked JC over and over if we could not hang with his friend as I was still weak with the drug, and his friend continued to smoke even on our boat at times. One last Saturday, it was a cold morning on the San Francisco Bay, and his friend had brought some coffee. I was freezing. He offered me the coffee, and I took several swallows of it. I instantly knew it had meth melted in it, but his friend failed to mention that. I instantly got warm all over and was in the middle of eating some crackers with peanut butter and got dry mouth; I could not eat anymore. JC drank the rest of the coffee, and we were both high instantly. We turned the boat around as it was dangerous, being high on the water! We got home, and we did not have any to smoke at this time, but what we ingested was enough to last the next four days. It had affected me a little differently ingesting it then smoking it. The visual and auditory hallucinations started much quicker for me. It was the most four awful days out of the year and a half.

We got home and did the usual sexual craziness and could not sleep. The auditory hallucinations were all about JC telling whoever I believe his ex-wife was that I was a horrible person, and as soon as I sober up, he is kicking me out and going back to her. Also, I was not a good candidate for the drug, and I was ruining the experience! I was so devastated, and JC wound up, locking me in the spare room and telling me to listen to music. I tried, but the voices came right through the loud music. It was awful as JC and I were trying to get back together, stay together, and get married! I was so convinced yet confused. On the following Monday, we had contractors coming to replace our floors in our bedroom, bathroom, and kitchen. By Monday, I was a total mess and had to deal with the contractors and the drills' noise as they put in tile floors and had to cut the tiles. The voices were crazy in my head the whole time. JC was getting so upset with me and yelling at me to stay in the room with the door closed. I was a prisoner in my own home. So much for doing drugs in a safe place.

I finally got some sleep and missed a few days of work again for the last time. When we both had enough sleep, I sat down with JC to talk about my experience. He thought it was just a hallucination and advised me to forget about it. I was devastated once again that he would not validate my hurt feelings and my crying for hours, begging for my sleep. I finally let him know I do forgive him and that it was time to move on.

We both promised that smoking must stop and got rid of all drug paraphernalia. I felt free for that moment. JC continued to bring his friend fishing, and I swear I got PTSD when I saw the drug paraphernalia on him. JC had a few hurtful comments. I felt so good being back at the gym. I was still smoking cigarettes, though, and was trying to quit. We spoke of the drug now and then which was okay until JC and I would try to have intimacy without the drug, and he would in the middle of the heated moments whisper in my ear, *"I wish we could go get the pipe and take a few hits."*

I would be so upset as our sex life became very scarce. It was never the same. I told JC one day that I had enough sex over the last year and six months to last a lifetime. Our lives returned to normal for a few months. We got some good sleep and began eating well again. We were both back to work. JC knew enough people to get another job with another company even after his decision to simply not show up.

We did have one friend who let us know as we sobered up that he almost called the cops to do a welfare check but did not want us both arrested, especially JC, as he already had a record and would do many years if caught.

Once again, I felt lucky not to have gotten caught in any way. JC then decided to get surgery for carpal tunnel and be home for six weeks recuperating. At that point, JC was home and bored while I was working. He became a little more possessive and insecure at the time. He would text all day, and I was busy and in meetings at times. He started to accuse me of cheating on him. He also went fishing a few times with his friend, and I was a little worried about the temptation of using meth during the six weeks he had off. He did not use but continued to harass me at work. I came home one day and let him know the wedding will be called off, and he needed to stop with the insecurity. He agreed on canceling the wedding as he would barely be back to work in July. I continued to see if JC would listen to my concerns, but he just couldn't let go of his insecure behavior.

Chapter 14
The Gypsy I am

I was already planning to leave, and I often began discussing my next move with my friends. I had a great friend Jerrie who offered me to share her apartment in a neighboring town. We both worked at the same place and so could carpool. I do have a habit of packing up and leaving before letting the other one know. Nonetheless, I have always warned them. As they say, men do not listen!

I was taken for granted in this relationship, and he thought I would never leave, especially after the drug use. It backfired and ruined us instead. I woke up one morning and did for what I had taken a day off. JC went off to work at about 5 am. I told him goodbye as I did every day. I could pack up in about 2 hours and make two trips to move all my stuff. I always kept my things packed light in case I needed to leave.

I started to pack my car and threw out many things as it was the "trash day." I threw all the sex toys and anything related to that drug time and was in Jerri's apartment by noon. The saddest part was leaving my rescue dog, Harley. He seemed very sad to watch me pack and leave. She knew something was wrong. I cried, leaving her. I hoped JC would keep her and take good care of her. Most of you would agree that you seel the true self of a person when you are leaving them. I texted JC that I had moved out. I also asked him not to contact me. I was weak and had gone back too many times in the past. Yes, you have guessed it right, he texted me back and called several times.

His reactions were typical. He got mean, called me names, and asked me to get rid of all pictures and videos we had made during our drug-time. I agreed to that anyway. He even wanted the part of the engagement ring he bought me. I bought the diamond, and he bought the outer part that was attached. I told him before I finally blocked him that I would return it in his mailbox when he was not home. I did not want to see him or communicate with him again. Not unless things calmed down in both our lives. There were too many hurt feelings involved. I could have let his family know why I had left but wanted JC to have the few family members he was left with to stay close to him. If they knew he involved me with his drug history, he might have been outed by his family. I always keep others' feelings in mind, even when leaving. We stopped communicating and let some time go. In the meantime, I kept my local job and had a fun summer with my friends. In the next six months, I was debating about moving to another area or state. I just felt I had finished my time there. I was there in Northern California for about seven years now. My son Kyle was still living in Colorado and was going to get married in December. It was nearing November of that year 2017. I was talking with my sister, who had relocated to Florida from New York. We discussed the possibility of me relocating there. She helped me find a job, and the position started in January 2018. I put in my notice and decided to start over in a new state.

It was an opportunity to get to spend time with my sister and start a new chapter. At this point, JC and I had not communicated for about six months. I wanted closure before I left. I sent him an email, and he agreed to meet for breakfast. We met in a very cordial manner, apologizing for hurting each other and agreeing to be friends. I believe closures are necessary for us to move forward in life; It helped me a great deal. I will admit it was hard not talking or seeing him at first, but it had to be done. I remained strong.

Kyle's Wedding

I decided to go to Florida after Kyle's wedding. Kyle's wife to be was from Southern California, and the wedding was to take place on a gulf course in Southern California. I then reunited with Lorna, my long time friend. We have known each other for about 30 years now. She lives in Southern California, and I went to stay with her and take her to Kyle's wedding. It had been years since she had seen him. Kyle's wedding was fabulous, small but so wonderful. As most know, there are a few very special days in a parent's life: the birth of a child, the wedding of your child, and the wonderful accomplishments along the way. Last but not least, Grandchildren that I am still waiting on!

Lorna and I enjoyed the wedding as we were the only two besides a few college friends and Kyle's Dad's family. His wife's family is much bigger, and she had most of the guests. We enjoyed dancing and the usual wedding festivities. I recorded their first dance, and still watch it occasionally with tears of joy. I watched my son with a great smile while he escorted his bride around during the reception. I cannot ever find the words to describe how proud I am of what a wonderful man he has grown up to be! I try to tell him often!

It was around Christmas time, which I spent time with Lorna and her friend Janet. Janet is the most wonderful giving person I had ever met, and she made Lorna so happy – they had both lost their partners in the last few years. I also spent part of Christmas day with Kyle and his new wife and her family. Kyle and his new bride Lauren went back to Colorado, where Kyle was finishing a 6-year contract with the Army.

I continued on a trip across the country to Florida to start my new job in January 2018. I enjoyed my five-day trip driving across the country. I even visited a friend Bonnie I had known for about 30 years as we met our ex-husbands here in the military. I stopped in Louisiana for a few days and caught up. I continued to Florida and stopped at another friend's house about eight hours away from my sister. We spent the night drinking and catching up. It was a Maine friend, and I got the opportunity to reconnect with him on that trip. I finally got to my sister's place. It is a very nice one-story home with a wide refreshing backyard. They also have a nice pool and jacuzzi for relaxation and cooling off as Florida really does get hot and humid. I was there in January, so it was not too bad.

I pulled up to my sister's house early evening and still had about four days until the start of my new job. I unpacked my car in a few hours. She had given me my own bedroom and bathroom. I unpacked and hung up clothes in the closet and settled in. I had a few days to get to know the area and find out where food markets, gyms, and nail places were. I enjoyed spending time with my sister and her husband. They showed me around and took me to a few beach areas.

My sister introduced me to a guy while I was there, and he took me to a military ball. I being prior military, have a great love for this institution. Anyhow, I had a great time with him there and even saw him a few times after that. My sister drove us on the first day of my new job as we worked at the same place. It was a telephonic nurse case manager position, which was of the government payroll. I had just worked for a government position and had credentials, so I had to start immediately. My credentials were just transferred over.

The job included working with the military officers to ensure they got their benefits or if they were in need. I was introduced to the Director, who was also from NY and had a nice personality. I was introduced to the staff and others I was going to work with in the building. My first impression of working in a cubicle with six other people all trying to talk on the phone at once seemed overwhelming as I came from a place with my own office most of the time.

The people in that area of the East Coast were a little different in their attitude and work ethic. As I was learning the job, I met people that were very negative and had a kind of bullying behavior. I knew I was not going to like that environment being used to working professionally but gave it some time. I continued to be in the area for about a month and decided I was going to go back to California.

I went into the office one day and spoke to the manager about how I just don't feel like I would be a great fit and needed to go back where I was more comfortable and had lived most of my life. She appreciated the honesty and understood. I did not share my decision with my sister right away as I knew she wanted me to stay wanting to know me a little better. We have lived on opposite sides of the country for decades and only saw each other a few dozen times over the years.

One Friday morning, while getting ready for work, I let my sister know that it was my last day. She was shocked and upset, and I understood why at the moment. I tried to explain that everyone has a different place of happiness, and mine was in California. She was hurt and wanted me to stay so we could get to know each other better. I explained it to her the kind of person I am. When I am not happy, I need to keep moving. I drove separately to work as I was leaving as soon as I could. I quietly left the building and ran some errands to get ready for the road trip back to California. I stayed with my sister for the weekend. We spent our final days visiting beach areas and sharing quality time. I packed my car again and headed out that following Monday morning into California in mid-January of 2018.

I was not sure where I was headed in California at first. I had many friends in Northern and Southern California; I had no current job lined up but knew something would come along. I had spoken to Lorna and Janet in Southern California, and they said I could stay with them as long as I needed and had a place to go. I was so excited as I wanted to reunite more with Lorna as we had lost touch. I then again took the 5-day trip back and enjoyed my time on the road.

Of course, I stayed with my friend Bonnie in Louisiana again on my way back. She was happy to see me and was not surprised as she knew me well to be a little gypsy soul that had relocated frequently over the years. I finally arrived back in California, unpacked, and settled in with Lorna and Janet. I started my journey of looking for a job in the area.

It was a few months, and I joined a gym, I was working out and keeping busy while I was applying for a nurse position. I continued to enjoy having fun with Lorna and Janet as they seemed like a combination of mother figures and college roommate friends. We all enjoyed the same fun things, such as casinos and going out to eat. We all enjoyed a few drinks and lots of laughs. We also had a lot of get-togethers at the house with friends and laughs. We went on a few trips as well. I would watch the house and cats as they went on a few trips together. The cats, I do need to take a moment to talk about the cats.

Lorna has three cats – Melaia, Thumbelina, and Tommy; they are between 12 and 13 years old. Janet has two younger cats, Charlie and Precious. These cats are the babies in the family and have brought great joy to all of us. I am never alone; I go home to a loving, caring family.

At this point, I continue to date online with no luck, and I am in and out of the dating scene over the years. I spoke with

Janet and Lorna about working at the facility Janet was working at, and Lorna had worked at years ago. I met up with the director at a job fair. I let her know I knew Janet, and she took my resume. A few days later, I had an interview and was hired. I was to be an RN supervisor of a 120 bed locked psyche facility. I had a psyche background as a nurse. I went through orientation and started a full-time day shift Monday through Friday. It was a unique place, and employees had longevity there, including Janet.

I had the opportunity to educate younger nurses; it was a little challenging as employees were very set in their ways with some willingness to learn. I realized quickly that this was short term employment due to salary and work environment. I knew I wanted much more for my own growth and had the experience and the time to go and do whatever my dreams were. I wanted to do some travel nursing again, as it always seems to fit my gypsy lifestyle, looking for a change and new experiences.

I started to reach out to a travel company and met a few recruiters to see where and what type of job would be a traveling one. I have been doing case management for several years at different levels. The recruiter put together a resume, and we put in for a few jobs up in Northern California. I let the Director know that I was looking for jobs and won't be there very long. She understood and knew I needed to expand my career and make money worthy of all my years of experience.

I was having a pedicure one day when I had an interview on the phone for a position in Northern California, and about 40 minutes later, I got a call for an offer for a 13-week assignment. I was so excited about the opportunity to do travel nursing, meet new people, and gain new experiences! I took the job and had a few weeks to prepare and get up to Northern California. I contacted my friend Phyllis up there that I had previously mentioned, and she said I was more than welcome to stay with her for the 13 weeks. I had decided to give her a monthly fee for the room rental; we both helped each other whenever we could.

Lorna and Janet were happy for me and my new adventure. I told them I would come to visit as often as I could, and in between assignments. I decided to travel up and down the coast of California for a few years as it paid well. Now, I have friends on both coasts. I also wanted to pay off all bills over the next 2-3, years including my current car.

The travel nursing journey began in September of 2018.

Chapter 15
Travel Nursing... to Mom!

I packed my car with needed clothing and shoes to start my new travel nurse assignment. I traveled the eight hours to Northern California to Phyllis's house. I arrived in the evening and unpacked into the room I was renting out. I knew Phyllis and her family well and enjoyed spending time with them. I settled into my new job at a very nice hospital and started meeting new friends and visiting the old ones. My first 13 weeks went extremely well. I did another assignment and continued to save money and really living out my dreams as planned.

It seemed surreal at first. I visited Lorna and Janet periodically while continuing to work and have fun with friends. I am living the dream and am very content with life.

Not everything has been perfect in these six months. I have recently learned that Lorna had cancer and that it had come back. I was devastated and wanted to be closer to her and Janet. Lorna also had a mini-stroke that did not leave any residual effects. Lorna wanted me to continue to work up north for now as it was newly diagnosed, and she had Janet. I did another three months, which seemed to have gone by fast as work was very busy. I met a wonderful friend who is also a marketing director for a facility named Cam, and I stayed with her for the last three months of my nine-month assignment in Northern California. She lived closer to the hospital, and I enjoyed spending time with her at the local downtown area for dinners and drinks.

I also spent significant time with a very cool couple who loved to have a good time and was very outgoing; they introduced me to their great group of friends. I had gone to Reno for a weekend with Cindy, and we clicked perfectly even on road trips. That is a hard friendship to find. My experiences and friendships took me to many places, but every experience is unique and inspirational. Whether the ones I've had or the ones' I will have in the future.

In the meantime, Kyle hurt his kidney in training; at first, I was devastated as I did not know the extent of the injury. Kyle had informed me he was in a barracks typesetting and receiving pain management until his team could get him back to Colorado to the Army hospital. I worried so much over the next few weeks. He finally was seen in Colorado and did have a blockage in the bladder, causing the pain. He had a minor surgery that seemed to clear up the issue. I was so relieved! Kyle was then thinking about getting out of the military and spending time with Lauren. Kyle got out of the military at the end of 2018 and started a Master's degree. He was thinking about going to Law school next. Lauren was in school, too, working on a radiology career.

I arrived home back with Janet and Lorna. Lorna was now having Pet Scans and was taking oral chemos. Gladly, she was doing well for the diagnosis. I took some time off in between assignments. I was interviewed to get an assignment in San Diego this time, which was only on an hour's drive from Lorna's place. I got hired within hours of the interview. My assignment started in August 2019. I started the first month by driving every night back and forth and was actually used to it. I was meeting new friends once again and learning new electronic health record applications for the new hospital. This assignment was a little different; I did not meet those friends out socially as I wanted to spend as much time with Lorna and Janet as possible. Also, the job and travel were stressful at times, and the time went fast. I also did not work weekends, so I had time to spend with

Lorna and Janet. We did fun stuff on weekends or just stayed home together. One Friday morning, I received a call from Barb, my sister, from NY. She was caring for my biological mother, Sharon, for the past several years on and off. She had been in the hospital and a rehab facility on and off over several months. She was currently in a hospital, and my sister Barb did not know what to do. I had told her years before to call me if anything happened or if Sharon became ill. I told her I would be there. The day had come for me to keep my word. I was at work getting ready to start my day.

I went to my supervisor and let her know that I was going on leave. My leadership team had already told me to go to NY and take care of business and take a week if I needed it. I was relieved that they understood. This was September 20, 2019. I got in the car, and it was an hour's drive home. I spoke with a few people on the way, including Barb, to let her know I was going to get an overnight flight and be there in the morning. My other sister in Florida, who is also a nurse, was flying in the next morning. I flew on that Saturday morning and got an Uber from the airport as my sister was working that day. My sister's wife greeted me at the small apartment my sister was living in, and it was only a mile away from the beach! It is a cute downstairs apartment that they rent from the owner upstairs. This was the place where my biological mother, Sharon, had been living. I could see the medical equipment such as oxygen around the apartment. My other sister arrived within hours of myself and had taken an Uber to the apartment as well. We visited and caught up while we waited for Barb to get home and take us to the hospital to see what was going on medically with Mom. Barb arrived, and we all went up to the hospital. We soon found out the medical issues and realized she was not doing well. She had pulmonary and respiratory issues, had oxygen on, and looked pale. She was alert enough to know we were there.

She looked at each of us and smiled under the oxygen mask. We, as a family, discussed and realized that we needed to talk with the physician. The physician had orders to do everything she could to save her life. Mom was alert enough for me to ask her about what she wanted, and she did want everything done, including CPR, if her heart had stopped. Each of us visited her for a while and then went home for the evening, leaving her to the medical team for the night. My other younger sister was deciding whether to come to NY or just wait and see what happened. I told her just to wait and that we would keep her posted. My brother, who is now in North Carolina that I have not seen since I was 12, was debating about coming to see her and us. It had been ages since we had seen him last. I also met another sister I had not met ever before. I came to know she was close to my Mom. She was taking her illness and condition very hard.

It was a Sunday, and I had been in NY for a few days. Barb and I were at the beach, which was a great place for serenity for us to figure out what to do. My sister from NY and I argued that morning, and she decided to go back to Florida that day instead of staying. I believe our argument was from stress from the situation, and she decided to go back home. I was staying all week anyway as planned. While on the beach, we received a call from the physician that my Mom had a rapid response this morning and had a collapsed lung. She then had a chest tube in! She also told us that she was not doing well, and we needed to get to the hospital and make some decisions.

We drove over to the hospital, and she took a turn for the worst and was not alert. We had our other sister I had not met as of yet come to the hospital as we needed to let her know how it was to be a DNR situation as she could not take another rapid response or code. At first, that sister was very upset and came to the hospital, thinking we could do more. She did not understand the disease process at all. I explained the situation in the best terms I could for someone with no medical background. We met with the physician to get a DNR and put her on Hospice. All treatment was stopped besides giving her the oxygen. We wanted to keep her comfortable and pain-free. They started a morphine drip by Sunday evening, and we stayed at the hospital. We watched her as she was getting ready to cross over, put her hands up, and yelling out, "I am trying to get there, Momma." It was actually really amazing to see.

Monday came, and we were all saying goodbye as she could still hear us, her sisters came by, and my sister from NY drove down to see her. My brother in NC could not afford to get there, so we did some face time with Mom for him. My sister from Florida had said goodbye a few days earlier when she was more alert. The staff nursing team there was pretty good but not very attentive as they knew I was a nurse and advocating for her every step of the way. It seemed there were new nurses in training at the time, and I was patient as I had been there years ago. I had over 29 years of experience under my belt. I understood and trained nurses myself over the years. They appreciated our patience through this time of our lives. A few examples of a teaching moment came with a respiratory therapist who was still trying to give a breathing treatment and had asked if I would give the treatment and turn it off afterward and put the oxygen mask back on. I was shocked that any person would ask a family member to give a medication! I lit into him a little bit about the discontinued treatments as she is on morphine and in the dying process, and family members are never to do such a thing! I let the charge nurse know, in case he did that to any other family member!

They responded back by saying, that is not okay! My sister Barb was so happy I was there because she had no clue how the situation had to be dealt with. By this time, we are up for a few days, it is hard to sleep in the hospital, and we did not want her to take her last breath alone. That has been my rule as a nurse for years; no one is to die alone! Another incident was where a nurse started another morphine drip and walked away; I noticed my Mom was getting restless and yelling out more in discomfort. I asked the nurse to check the IV, and it was not going in as the nurse had forgotten to open the line. She was standing at the bedside, trying to figure it out; I pointed out the issue. She fixed it and apologized, and even though we had little to no sleep over the last few days, we were again very patient. The staff had to be asked to please change all the bedding and clean up my Mom; I believe they were thinking of just leaving us alone during this time. I assisted with a few bed changes, and the body fluids were seeping from my Mom, and she really needed to be clean and dry. At this point, she was not urinating much, and her kidneys were shutting down. I assisted with the changes in linens.

The days and nights seemed to be running into each other. We were laughing and crying over everything due to lack of sleep. I kept checking on my sisters as we all watched our mother's dying process as they had never experienced it like this. They understood and did well, so it seemed. I may not have known how much they were hurting inside. I sure was but always tried to be the strong one. It was now Monday night at about 11 pm, and it seemed her breathing was slowing down with the morphine drip. She seemed much more comfortable, and so the yelling out had ended. We were all kind of quiet and trying to get a few minutes of sleep. I then looked up and realized she still had the 10 liters of oxygen going, and I took it off as planned when she settled down. When the oxygen was removed, she had passed within 2 hours about 1:15 am on Tuesday morning September 24, 2019. We then saw the last breath, and I went to let the nurse know. The nurse came in and wasn't sure; she went to get a doppler to feel if there was any heartbeat. Now we were so tired and just wanted to go home and get some sleep. I said, "Are you kidding? She is gone"! I believe she may have never seen a person pass away! After a few minutes, she decided that she was gone.

Then the weirdest thing happened! There was a machine that had vital signs recorded, and my sister, who has no medical background, noticed that the heart rate was 134. "Who's heart rate is that?" We busted out laughing at the oddest moment, but it was explained that recording was from earlier. We had talked about a funeral home in the area, and she wanted to be cremated. I then asked the nurse if they called the funeral home, as most hospitals did. She let me know it is up to us to pick the place and call ourselves. I was so tired and said, "Okay, we are not sure yet, can you keep her overnight while we get some sleep?" I could not believe we had to call ourselves. I was just in a strange place and hoped my sister who lived there could recommend something. We decided to go home, get sleep, and worry about it in the morning as my mother was not going anywhere until she was picked up. We were relieved she passed peacefully, and we were there with her.

We got to my sister's place about 2 in the morning, exhausted beyond words, and took a long-needed hot shower. We slept for 10 hours. It was just the beginning of much-needed sleep, and I still had the rest of the week off. We all woke up, and my sister from upstate NY went home. Barb and I went over to the funeral home. It seemed so weird to me to be walking up to a funeral home and asking them to go pick up our mother and cremate her. We walked up to the funeral home, it had tall 10 feet doors, and we rang the bell-like we were visiting someone at their home! We saw someone open the curtain on a side window and motion us to go around to a different door! We finally got inside, and they agreed to pick our Mom up and do the cremation. It certainly was a weird feeling inside the funeral home, as most of us know, since we have all been there to see a loved one leave us forever at some point. We paid for the pick up of our mother. It was like 500 dollars, and Barb and I were joking that maybe we should get her and bring her over ourselves. We were still exhausted and punchy at this time. We paid for the services and left the funeral home. I enjoyed the time spent with my sister for the rest of the week as she was able to take time off and spend with me. We enjoyed the beach.

We went to lunch several times, the beach every day, and slept and slept. The day had come when I needed to get back to California and back to my job! My sister dropped me off at the airport, and I took the long journey and a few layovers from NY to California. I got home and had Sunday to enjoy the day with my roommates Lorna and Janet. Monday morning arrived, and I started my drive back to San Diego to finish out my travel assignment until November 2, 2019. The workplace was so warm and welcoming, not realizing my Mom had passed. They also paid for the day I left early after the news.

I settled back into my routine and got busy with life. I felt good that I had done the right thing even though I had not seen her for quite a while. All that matters is she knew I was there for her at the end and made it comfortable for her. It was the end of a chapter, seeing off my mother, knowing she is now in a better place. I had fun over the weekends with Lorna and Janet as we liked to go out to eat, have drinks, and make memories. We also enjoyed several casinos in the area and went often. My travel assignment ended, and I had two months off for the holidays. It meant it was time to finish writing this book. I went up to Northern California to visit some friends for about 12 days. I saw some significant friends, Sharon was one who I spent time with their family throughout the last eight years. We visited and went out with friends and had a great time. That family is an example of great love and happiness, and I always enjoy their company.

I moved on to another friend Cindy and James, who enjoy life to the fullest as I do, and that's why we connect. I stayed with them for five days or so and went to our old stomping grounds to see friends I had known up there. I also stopped at the hospital I worked at up there to see all my nursing friends there. We went out to dinner a few times. Then I went on to see Jerry, my old roommate, who took me in when JC and I broke up, or should I say when I left JC. We enjoyed watching our favorite shows together and went to a casino there that we both liked. As you see, there is a trend here. I love casinos wherever I go. The thing is I am disciplined with my money and limit every time I find myself at a poker table. I do not mix drinking and gambling to a point where I don't know what money I am spending. We could say I am better at gambling than drinking as far as control is concerned! I then flew out and returned home in Southern California to get busy with this book and enjoy the holidays!

Chapter 16
Until Next Time

It was a couple of weeks of being home. I was moving along swiftly with the book and relaxation. I also had joined a winery and went a few times with some new friends I had made. Lorna was going to her appointments, and Janet and I were worried about her as she was battling cancer. We still continued to have fun as long as Lorna had the energy.

One day Lorna seemed short of breath, having very little energy. We thought it was the side effect of the chemo meds. Her weakness seemed to go on for too long, so finally, Janet took her to an appointment she had. She was hospitalized with blood clots in her lungs, which can be fatal if not treated. We were so happy to have caught it. She received her treatment in time, spending only a few days at the hospital. Janet spent the days and nights with her there. Janet and Lorna have a special bond; they do everything together!

I remember visiting Lorna in the hospital. She has a fantastic way of dealing with her illness. She always stays positive, which is what half of the battle is. She was released, and we were finally all home together again, trying to get back to normal. Lorna healed, and her breathing returned to normal; she no longer needed oxygen. We were now heading towards Thanksgiving, and we decided to stay home and keep Lorna away from too many germs excusing the friend who had invited us for Thanksgiving. For Christmas, we started to decorate the house and even put some lights on the house out front. Janet and I were putting the strands of lights up. It was a cold day, and both of us were laughing and freezing, trying not to tangle the lights. We got a few strands up, and they looked beautiful. They were white lights and had three different functional modes of blinking. Janet put it on multi-mode.

One evening, as usual, Janet went to bed earlier than us because she worked early hours and was always home by early afternoon as she got to spend time with Lorna. Lorna is Janet's favorite person and loves to spend time with her. They went on trips together and just enjoyed each other's company. I have the pleasure of knowing them and witnessing the love they shared. I consider them my Moms, and that's how I describe them to my friends. Anyway, back to that evening, Janet had been in the bedroom for maybe 15 minutes, and she started screaming out. She was in a lot of pain and started to vomit violently, turned red, and was really in pain. Janet told us it was her stomach that had the pain on one side. She kept yelling and vomiting. She would try to lay down again, and it would not stop. We asked her if she could get in the car and we would take her to the ER. She was not strong enough to get to the car, so we called 911.

The ambulance arrived, and the paramedics took her vital signs. To no surprise, her blood pressure and heart rate were very high, and she had an erratic heartbeat. We met her at the hospital as she was taken away in the ambulance. Lorna was able to go back with her, and I was in the waiting room. The ER was so busy that she was in the hallway of the ER and having blood work and tests done. They sent Janet home that night and said it was colitis with inflammation of the colon. She continued to be in pain and very uncomfortable for the next few days and really could not eat anything. Lorna took her back to the hospital, and she was finally admitted.

This was a few days before Thanksgiving, so we knew she was not going to be home by the holiday. We had a few friends over every year, but this time we decided to cancel that holiday and just do it when Janet got better. I ordered the dinner already prepared, and a few friends came over after we had visited Janet on Thanksgiving morning. Janet was still in pain and not doing well. Her color was pale, she was not tolerating food, and the pain seemed worse. She was given pain meds in the hospital, but it seemed they weren't helping. Lorna was advocating for her every day, and they kept saying no to surgery. I went home and prepared the already cooked dinner and picked up some pies. It was definitely a weird Thanksgiving without Janet. Janet had insisted Lorna to leave for home to have dinner. Lorna felt bad, but she needed to eat and get sleep as she was battling her own illness. She did well during these weeks of Janet in the hospital despite her lack of sleep and worrying about Janet. She stayed day and night and came home to sleep in her own bed now and then.

Christmas was coming around, and the hospital kept giving Janet pain pills that eventually made her have delirium and hallucinate. It was very hard for us to see her like that. She was begging us to help with the pain. We brought up surgery several times, and they felt it was not necessary. Janet even had a nasogastric tube to give her intestines rest. She eventually pulled that out, and they started giving her a liquid diet. She only took sips of broth a day. She was losing weight from not eating. She had diarrhea for several days, and we thought that maybe it was a bowel obstruction. The doctors prescribed cat scans and MRIs. Upon receiving the reports, they concluded that there was no obstruction. Christmas came and went. I saw Kyle and Lauren over the holiday. They saw Lorna but did not visit Janet in the hospital as she did not want too many visitors to see her like that. I took Kyle and Lauren to the winery; we had lunch and spent the day together. It was great to see them; they are my pride and joy in life! They enjoyed visiting Lorna and me.

I was also interviewing for my next travel nursing assignment and decided to stay in Lorna and Janet's area. It was the plan all along to stay in Southern California for a while with them. After all, it was my home too. I interviewed for a position nearby and got the job. I was to start on January 6, 2020. In the meantime, Janet was still in the hospital. The month of January 2020 arrived. I was getting ready to start my new position. It was January 4 when the doctors decided that Janet needed surgery. I was heading over to the hospital when I received a text from Lorna letting me know that Janet had just come out of surgery and that it was not good news. She was in ICU and on life support. My heart and stomach sunk, and I did not know what to say. She also asked me not to call her as she did not have the strength to talk to anyone. It turned out they had to remove most of her lower intestines, and if she was to come through, she would need nutrition through her veins and would not be able to eat by mouth for the rest of her life. She also might have to have a colostomy and urostomy bag, and for those who don't understand what that is, it is a way of eliminating urine and bowel movements but through a bag hanging off each side of your body. Also, her kidneys were failing rather quickly.

I got to the hospital and met up with Lorna in the waiting room of the ICU. They were settling Janet in before visitors could see her. Lorna and I spoke in the waiting room, and we were discussing if Janet could beat this, we would be there for her every step of the way. Finally, we were able to see her. Lorna and I walked into the ICU into her room, and I lost any patience I had. It was painful to see her that way hooked up to life support. I felt so helpless for Lorna. She had just lost her husband John a few years ago. It was heartbreaking to see her at Janet's bedside. We were waiting for Norette, Lorna's childhood friend. Norette had been there for her over the years, including her battle with cancer and John's death. The physician told us that she was not doing well, and we needed to consider her quality of life if she made it through. At first and all the way until the end, Lorna had much hope.

Finally, after about 24 hours, Lorna realized a decision had to be made. Lorna decided on Monday, January 6, 2020, to take off the life support. If Janet pulled it through on her own, we were to get our answer. Lorna wanted to be alone with Janet for such an intimate time for two people who are so in love. Norette and I waited in the ICU waiting room and gave Lorna her time with Janet. It was about 5 minutes or less, and Janet had passed away. The answer was Janet did not pull through, and Lorna felt she made the right decision. We spent some time to say goodbye to Janet. I left and let Lorna take her time; she needed to say goodbye.

Lorna came home that day in the early evening, and I did not know what to say. I would wait for the moments she would mention Janet, and then I would join in and tell her how sorry I was that she lost her love. Lorna is the strongest woman I know, and she has been a great role model and a mother figure to me, and now I find myself spending quality time with her and trying to console her when appropriate. The next day Lorna and Norette went to the funeral home to set arrangements for Janet to be cremated as were her wishes. I finally started my 13-week travel nurse assignment locally. I was happy to be staying local and spend time with Lorna and be here for her. I usually am not home every night, but it seemed it was meant to be at this time of our lives. My ultimate plan was to spend time with Lorna and Janet, and I am grateful for the time we had together as I consider them my family! The new assignment seems a bit different than my other assignments. It is a brand new hospital and has a great staff in the case management department.

Due to budget constraints, as they say, we seem to be working for short staff and doing more work than I am used to doing. In other hospitals, we had case manager assistants, and here we, the nurses, are doing all administrative and discharge planning. It is not my favorite place to work, but after two months off and the unexpected death of Janet, I needed a distraction. Of course, my bank account also needed some rebuilding. We tried to get back to life without

Janet in it, and it has been a challenge even for the cats in the house. Animals, as most of us know, have a sense of loss when a person is not around anymore. Janet's cat Precious who is approximately two years old still to this day waits by the door to see if Janet will walk through the door. We all have our sadness over Janet's death, especially Lorna. I believe we all grieve differently and at our own pace. Lorna picked up the ashes of Janet and had bought a beautiful wooden box to put her ashes in. Janet always loved wooden boxes. As I am writing this story and finishing this book until the next volume comes out, Janet is in the wooden box in front of me, telling me everything will be okay. She is also telling me to make sure that I look after Lorna as she looks after both of us!

In the meantime, I had been going out socially with new friends in the area. I met a really nice gentleman and his best friend while out having lunch and a few drinks at the local bar and grill. It is also a place I am known to have been dancing on a few Saturday nights to the band. The music is usually a country which I love, but it is occasionally rock and roll. The handful of times I had been there dancing has been very fun. I love to go out dancing every few months or so. Anyway, I came into the restaurant and sat at the bar, ordered a drink. It did not take me long to notice three people to my left talking. It was a woman and two guys. After a while, they said hello, and we started talking. The female was pretty drunk, and they were letting me know they had met a few weeks ago at that restaurant. I started talking with them, and then the female decided she had to go, and we tried to get an Uber for her, but she refused. We stayed in the evening, and eventually, my new guy friend came over and sat next to me. His friend was talking with others as the dinner hour was approaching. Well, we had been there since 2 pm!

I was enjoying the company of this gentleman. I am used to guys approaching me with more aggression and wanting me to have sex at the end of our conversing and having a few drinks. I recently had come off all dating sites in the last few months, trying to meet people more safely. All my friends say that you meet a nice guy when you least expect it. I believe I finally did!!! So we talked about life and before we knew it his friend left for the evening and it was just him and I. I asked the bartender when does the band start and what type of music they played. The band started at 8:30 pm, and it was to be country music. When I asked, it was only 6 pm! We decided to stay for the music, drink some more and have dinner. We were both getting a little tipsy but having a great time. Then the music started. We danced and danced to slow songs and fast ones. We held each other during slow dances and even kissed on and off. We stopped drinking liquor and just danced for the last few hours on nothing but water. We closed the place down, and my guy friend said he never did that before! I let him know if he wanted to hang with me, we might do it again sometime. He drove me home as I could not safely drive, kissed, and went into the house to fall asleep. The next day he texted to see how I was doing, and I let him know I was a little hungover but was out running errands.

He had a headache but was out shopping with his nephews. He currently lives with his brother and his nephews. He is a great uncle and a role model for the kids, at least, from how I see him. Over the next few weeks, he texted me now and then. I was busy at work, working overtime on most days. I did not answer him for days. It was not on purpose; it's just that I did not want to give him the wrong idea at the time that we may become a couple. I am so used to being single now that honestly when a nice guy comes along, I shy away at first. He finally asked in a text if he did something to offend me, and I felt bad and let him know I was just busy. He also kept texting about meeting up again. Then within a week, I invited him to lunch and a drink. We met at another neighborhood restaurant. We both started to talk about our first night. He said his brother wanted to meet me. I said that I would love to meet his brother and nephews sometime. He was stating he thought the first night he might have been out of line or forward about holding and kissing me during our slow dances. He even had a video of me dancing! I said I thought I was a little forward, so we both decided it was okay on both ends.

He said he just wanted someone he could spend time with, and I agreed as I wanted the same. I had an appointment to get my nails done, and he jokingly said to put his initials on my valentine nails. Guess what! I did it! We met up later after the nail appointment at our original place of meeting. We met up again that day. We were talking and eating on just another Saturday night. We joked that we were not staying and dancing again until closing! We both agreed, and he walked me to my car, we kissed, and both drove home for the evening. I continue to work at the local hospital and come home in the evening to Lorna. We watch our favorite shows together. We speak of Janet often in conversation, and she remains with us in the living room, watching over us from heaven. I have a date this coming weekend, which is valentine's weekend, to take my friend to the winery as he has never been to one. He has no idea who I am and the fun and joy we can have together if it is meant to be. I will take it one day at a time and see where it leads. This year of 2020, I need to do a lot of things, including travel, fun, and meeting a few of my biological siblings. I will continue to love my family and friends, make new friends, and continue my adventures wherever they take this gypsy soul.

I hope whoever gets to read my story learns a few things from it. I am a survivor, not a victim of the broken foster care system. All my friends and family reading this, I love you all dearly, and thank you for taking this journey with me. You may now know me better and maybe understand me better. If you enjoyed this journey, stay tuned for the next chapter of my journey to hopefully find love and be a Grandmother, which will be my greatest joy ever besides my son Kyle! Stay tuned, and see you all in the next book!